ALL MINE

by

Noel Cashford MBE RNVR

with illustrations by

Noel Cashford

© Noel Cashford MBE 2002

Illustrations by Noel Cashford

Printed and published by:
ALD Design & Print
279 Sharrow Vale Road
Sheffield S11 8ZF

Telephone 0114 267 9402
E:mail a.lofthouse@btinternet.com

ISBN 1901587231

First published July 2002

All rights reserved
No part of this publication may be reproduced, stored in a retrieval system or transmitted in any form or by any means, electronic, mechanical, photocopying, recording or otherwise, without the written permission of the publisher.

All views and comments printed in this book are those of the author and should not be attributed to the publisher.

Other titles in the series

Mi-Amigo - The Story of Sheffield's Flying Fortress	David Harvey	ISBN 1-901587-00-2
Tales From a Peak District Bookshop	Mike Smith	ISBN 1-901587-01-0
Tha' Don't look Proper - Girl with cleft palate & hare lip	Anne Hunt	ISBN 1-901587-02-9
Shiny Sheff - The Story of Sheffield's Fighting Ships	Alistair Lofthouse	ISBN 1-901587-03-7
Doug's War - An Erksome Business - War life story	Doug Sanderson	ISBN 1-901587-04-5
The Dramatic Story of The Sheffield Flood	Peter Machan	ISBN 1-901584-05-3
Carl Wark - Peak District Fortress or Folly?	Mick Savage	ISBN 1-901587-06-1
Then & Now - Sheffield	Alistair Lofthouse	ISBN 1-901587-07-X
Charlie Peace, The Banner Cross Murderer	Peter Machan	ISBN 1-901587-08-8
Then & Now - The Sheffield Blitz	Alistair Lofthouse	ISBN 1-901587-09-6
They Lived in Sharrow and Nether Edge	Nether Edge N'hood Group	ISBN 1-901587-10-X
Discovering Derbyshire's White Peak	Tom Bates	ISBN 1-901587-11-8
Lost Sheffield - Portrait of a Victorian City	Peter Machan	ISBN 1-901587-12-6
The Sheffield Flood - Large format for schools	Peter Machan	ISBN 1-901587-13-4
The Sheffield Outrages, The Trade Union Scandals	Peter Machan	ISBN 1-901587-14-2
A Layman's Look at the History, Industry, People and Places of Oughtibridge Worrall and Wharncliffe Side	Doug Sanderson	ISBN 1-901587-15-0
Derbyshire in Old Photographs	E Mottram & A Lofthouse	ISBN 1-901587-16-9
Weerz me dad? 40s & 50s Childhood Stories	Fred Pass	ISBN 1-901587-17-7
'Orreight mi Ol?' Observations on Sheffield Dialects	Don Alexander	ISBN 1-901587-18-5
Sheffield Woodland Detectives - Large Format for Schools	Joan & Mel Jones	ISBN 1-901587-19-3
The Story of the Workhouse and Hospital at Nether Edge	Joan Flett	ISBN 1-901587-20-7
More By Luck Than Judgement	Prof. Roy Newton	ISBN 1-901587-21-5
Memories of the Workhouse & Hospital at Fir Vale	Lyn Howsam	ISBN 1-901587-22-3

About the Author

Noel Cashford was born in Royal Tunbridge Wells, Kent where, as a boy, he was an active member of the Navy Leagues Sea Cadet Corps. At the outbreak of war he volunteered and became a member of LDV (Local Defence Volunteer) force which later became the Home Guard. He recounts some of the incidents with which he was involved during that time. In 1941 he volunteered to join the Royal Navy as Ordinary Seaman being posted to HMS Pembroke, Chatham.

After getting some sea time he was recommended for Officer Training. After passing at the Greenwich Naval College he was commissioned as a Sub Lieutenant RNVR Special Duties. He joined a relatively small band of officers who were trained to render safe unexploded bombs, sea mines and, in fact, any unexploded device found in sea and shore surroundings. He was trained to dive using an Admiralty pattern diving suit (heavy gear) and later with the frogman suit unit. Diving was, he admits, his most disliked task.

When he was demobilised in 1947, he remained a member of the Supplementary Reserve, for a very short period attached to HMS Wessex based at Southampton. After becoming a salesman, manager and area manager for a national company he then became group training officer until retirement. Whilst with his employer he lectured socially to various associations, mainly about bombs and mines. It was one of these early talks that stimulated the development of his visual presentations.

Since his retirement he has presented "All Mine" to various associations such as Round Table, Rotary Clubs, Luncheon Clubs, Probus Clubs, WI's, etc. He waives his fee and asks instead for a donation to be sent to Cancer Research or to Weston Park Cancer Care Hospital, Sheffield.

Author's Notes

I am grateful to my wife Brenda for spending many hours word processing this book and in jogging my weakening memory about incidents which, at the time, were nerve wracking.

Much of the material came as a result of her hoard of newspaper cuttings which were collected by her or were sent to her by grateful gentlemen of the press following the lifting of censorship after VE Day (Victory in Europe).

Alas, many photographs (some of which are shown throughout the book) have aged badly, mostly due to the glue available at the time.

I have refrained from giving precise dates and names of individuals because some items may invoke sad or unpleasant memories, also due to the passing years and a deteriorating ability to accurately recall details.

The following chapters are not chronological, but rather as remembered.

Press Cutting Acknowledgements

Daily Express

Daily Mail

Daily Mirror

Folkestone & Hythe Herald

Evening Standard

War Illustrated

1939 - 1948

Contents

	Page
In the Beginning	1
Memoirs of a Naval Bomb & Mine Disposal Officer	3
Home Guard (or LDV) UXB	5
My Story Begins in 1942	7
Frogmen?	8
The Case of the Missing Hammock	10
Rosneath Combined Operations Group	11
Adventure at Calshot Spit	13
Officer Training School	14
AA HQ Fanum House, The Aldwych, London	15
Journey Into a Strange New World	17
Boobies	20
The Day I Saw a Submarine	21
By the Book	23
Demolished!	26
Lady Luck Rock - Island of Tiree	29
Flying Again with the R.A.F	31
Incident at Ardrossan	34
Deadly Butterflies	36
Orange Galore or I Wasn't Lucky Enough To Get Whisky!	37
Initiation into Diving	40
More Diving	43
Even More Diving	45
Refreshers	47
Smoke Screen in Plymouth Docks	48
"D" Day 1944	50
Dredger Drama	51
Studland Battle Range	54
Stars & Stripes	56
Dangerous Cricket	58
Battle Ranges - Torcross and Starpoint 1945	62

Mount Wise	64
Target - Channel Islands	66
The Day St. Helier Nearly Blew Up	69
Jersey, Channel Islands	71
Bombs "On the Rocks"	74
Was there a Body in the Bag???	76
The Magpie Syndrome	78
End of Bachelor Days	79
Return to HMS Volcano	80
The Channel Tunnel - 1945	81
Hastings Harbour	83
1914 - 1948 Mine	85
Dredger - Dover Harbour	86
Dungeness 1945	90
Penny-Wise!	92
A Lobster's Catch	94
Pluto	96
Civic Reception ~ Hastings	98
Littlestone on Sea	100
The New Romney Mystery	103
Fisherman's Surprise Catch	105
St. Margaret's Bay	108
What The Papers "Cooked" Up	111
Lost in Norfolk	113
Unfair Criticism or One Rocket I Didn't Deserve!	115
Destiny?	117
Gales in the Channel - Autumn 1945	121
The Lost Weekend	125
Buckingham Palace	128
Dark Clouds Ahead	129
Life in Civilian Clothes	130
Memory Jogged	131
It's All Mine	133
1987	134
1995 Jersey Force 135	135

In the Beginning

Dear Reader, it will probably help you if I start by giving a potted history of my early life.

Just before war was declared in 1939 I left school and went to work as a trainee in a small electrical business in Tonbridge, Kent. I thoroughly enjoyed the work because of the variety. Most of our electricians were soon called into the forces, this meant I had to learn the skilled jobs very quickly.

The boss, James G.S. a super person and only just married to an equally super young lady, was very soon called to colours, leaving me, with James G.S's mother (another very nice lady) who came from Tunbridge Wells, to virtually run the business. During this time I cycled from the other side of Tunbridge Wells to Tonbridge, six days a week, 8.30 in the morning until 7.00 in the evening most nights. Having said this I really enjoyed the job.

On Tuesday and Saturday afternoons I was a keen member of the Navy League Sea Cadets Corps, rising to the dizzy heights of Leading Seaman Cadet. Then the war came to us. German raids came daily, their targets being London and airforce flying fields nearby. Frequent dog fights between the gallant Spitfire and Hurricane pilots and the best of the German Luftwaffe occurred, often right over head. Many on both sides being shot down, the lucky ones came down on parachutes. I witnessed many of these, close up or distant in the Weald of Kent. My admiration for the RAF and Allied pilots was unlimited.

My mother at home did her bit. In our modest home, she gave hospitality and a warm welcome to Canadian soldiers stationed nearby. She also made sure that every morning I was sent off to work having had a good breakfast. In retrospect, she must have given up her own rations to keep me well fed. When one is young these facts do not even register.

Soon I volunteered to join the newly formed Volunteer Defence Force (LDV), the forerunner of "Dad's Army"! At nineteen I volunteered to join the Royal Navy. I was accepted and arrived at HMS Pembroke at Chatham a few weeks later. My mother, who had been widowed when I and my twin were 18 months old, was then alone. My eldest brother was in the Middle East, in the Tank Corps with Montgomery, fighting Rommel. My sister was in the WAAF at RAF HQ in London as Flight Sergeant (Transport). Twin brother Jack was in the RAF in Canada learning to be a pilot. So you can see my mother considered she was doing 'her bit' for the war effort.

Now I must tell you about 'wonder dog'. Because my mother was alone, my London based sister went to Battersea Dogs Home and obtained a beautiful Alsatian dog by name Bruce, which she presented to a very reluctant mother.

It did not take very long for the pair to be absolutely inseparable. She walked miles to ensure Bruce had his daily horseflesh, she trained him to do clever tricks, including 'un-armed combat', (woe betide anyone who raised an arm near Mother). There was more, Bruce was trained to rescue Mother.

When the sirens sounded during the frequent air raids, Mother and Bruce would rush to their cosy mattress under the stairs. There was always food and drink available for Bruce and, I suspect, a tipple for Mother. Sometimes air raids would last all night, Bruce was always ready for the role he had to play in the event of Mother needing rescue. Mother wore a thick leather belt round her waist, and on command Bruce would gently place his big jaws around the belt and proceed to drag 11 stone Mother from under the stairs into the living room. She claimed that Bruce never hurt her in the slightest.

In the eight weeks of initial training at Chatham I was able to get home often. In a very short time Bruce and I were also inseparable. He always whimpered in a special way when I had to leave for Chatham.

Sadly, after two years, Bruce developed distemper, a killer for dogs in those days, so we lost him and everybody in the family was devastated by this loss. He was only a young dog and we had hoped for many years of pleasure together, but it was not to be.

Memoirs of a Naval Bomb & Mine Disposal Officer

War was going badly for Britain. By the end of November 1939, just three months after hostilities began, we had lost: the Aircraft Carrier HMS Courageous, sunk by U-29; HMS Triton, a relatively new T class submarine tragically torpedoed by another British submarine; HMS Oxley. Only the Captain and two crewmen of the Triton survived. In the cold North Sea HMS Spearfish, an older submarine, was damaged by the Home Fleet which comprised the battleships Rodney, Nelson, Hood and Renown. The Royal Oak was later sunk at her moorings in Scapa Flow by U-47 captained by Lieutenant Prien.

The Armed merchant cruiser Rawalpindi was sunk in the North Atlantic by the German pocket battleship Scharnhorst who, with her sister ship Gneisenau, had managed to break through the British blockade and was roaming the seas looking for victims. HMS Nelson, the flagship of the Home Fleet, touched off a mine whilst entering the harbour and was damaged so severely she was out of action for many months. HMS Belfast, a brand new cruiser, had her keel ripped out by a magnetic mine during an attack by U-21.

On the 9th October, Lieutenant Johannes Haberkost in U-31 penetrated Loch Ewe and laid 18 mines. These were the first mines to be laid by a submarine. This will give the reader some indication of just how badly things were going for Britain in the early days of the war.

The night of 6/7th November was clear, the stars were bright and the usual veil of mist hung over the sea off the east coast of England. Lieutenant Commander Baron von Vanganheim in the German destroyer Hans Lody was conning his way into the shipping lanes just off Cromer. Following was a second destroyer the Erich Giese. It was 0205 hrs (five minutes past 2 am) when the Happisburgh Lighthouse was sighted a mere three miles distant. On the after deck of the destroyer mine laying experts were hard at work preparing their charges. The mines stood in two long rows on rollers and rails and at exactly 0212 hrs, one after the other rolled over the stern and splashed into the cold North Sea. After two normal contact mines would go a third, a very different one: Hitler's first secret weapon, the magnetic mine.

By the 22nd November German destroyers had visited the east coast shipping lanes eleven times, the Thames Estuary four times, Cromer three times, twice to the Humber and twice to the Tyne. During these unmolested visits they laid 828 mines, one third of which were magnetic. As a result of these activities the British destroyer HMS Blanch was the first victim of a magnetic mine and the second was HMS Gipsy. She was sunk just off Harwich.

One hundred and twenty eight ships were sunk around our coasts between September 1939 and March 1940, many within sight of land and some within reach of harbour. The shallow waters around our coast were a graveyard for ships. Many settled on the sea bed leaving their superstructures and masts as headstones. There was much jubilation throughout the Third Reich. The victorious German Navy were feted everywhere, in every biergarten and in every village, town and city.

The Head of the Luftwaffe, Reichmarshal Herman Goring, was extremely jealous of Naval achievements and was determined to share the glory by proposing the dropping of thousands of mines by aircraft in British harbours and waterways. Fortunately for this country, Grand Admiral Raeder of the German Navy resisted strenuously, but finally agreed to use naval aircraft to lay mines in shallow waters near important installations. In the meantime, Herman Goring was accumulating 2000 mines of various types ready for launching by the Luftwaffe as well as having aircraft converted and crews trained for mine laying operations in the future.

Our fortunes took a turn for the better on the night of 20th November when nine Heinkel seaplanes, on their first ever mine laying operation, came to the Thames Estuary. Of the nine that took off only four reached the target area. The others were forced to return to their base due to navigational error or mechanical problems. On this first visit seven mines were laid. On the second and third visits 24 were laid, mostly in the Thames Estuary and off Harwich. It was on the third visit at 22.00 hrs on the night of 22nd November that an incident occurred that was to prove decisive for the whole German mine laying programme.

Members of the Royal Observer Corps who were stationed on the foreshore near Shoeburyness sighted one of the German seaplanes in the dark, heavily clouded sky. It was lining up for a drop. As they watched they saw two objects leave the aircraft, two parachutes opened and two splashes occurred in the water. The Observers took accurate bearings and were aware that whatever had dropped into the water, come low tide would be high and dry. The local army garrison was alerted and two hours later they could see two large torpedo shapes lying on the mud on which they mounted guard.

At HMS Vernon, Portsmouth the Headquarters of Naval Bomb & Mine Disposal, Commander Ouvry was alerted and accompanied by Lieutenant Commander Lewis, dashed through the night to the scene. Together they performed the dangerous task of rendering safe these unknown weapons which turned out to be magnetic mines, Britain had captured her biggest and most important prize since the outbreak of hostilities. Commander Ouvry was awarded the OBE for his bravery that night.

Home Guard (or LDV) UXB

We were always on duty together, Bert and I. He was a man in his forties and I was 17 but we made a good team. This particular night we were on duty on the top of St Paul's Church tower. A red alert had commenced hours earlier and a few German bombers had passed overhead towards London. The night was dark with some high cloud.

Bert had been telling some of his yarns. He could tell a good story with great humour. Half way through the watch the wind increased and it was almost impossible to sit on the peak of the tower so we slid down to sit on the parapet which was about three feet higher than the lead flashed gutter. He scanned the sky to the east and south and I to the north and west. A bomber could be heard changing direction, it also seemed to be losing height, then we heard the unmistakable scream of falling bombs which seemed to be falling right over us. We crouched even lower and put our hands over our ears and waited for the bangs ..... they didn't come.

Picking up our field telephone we called the Home Guard post. The call was answered by a sleepy sounding corporal. We told him that somewhere nearby several bombs had fallen but not exploded, upon which he asked if we had been asleep as he hadn't heard any aircraft. Shortly however, the sentry on duty at the school gates went to report hearing bombs falling. A runner on a bicycle was despatched to the nearest ARP post to report the incident and a small patrol was sent out into the surrounding common land to try to spot the unexploded bombs.

In the meantime, we were relieved by the next watch on the tower. It was our time to be off duty, have a cup of hot tea and try to catch a few hours sleep. The corporal came as we were finishing our tea. He apologised and said we would have to go on the Highrocks patrol as he was convinced we would have German parachutists landing this night. These bombs had been dropped as decoys he thought. Our steps were those of tired men as we had both been on the go for 22 hours non-stop having done a twelve hour stint at work.

Our rifles weighed tons but it was the excess of humour from Bert that kept me going. It was 5 am, dawn was just breaking and there was only another mile or so to go and no aircraft could be heard. We approached a private road. On the right were some very large houses which were occupied by the Army. On the road ahead lay a dark shape. As we approached it was identifiable as a very large German bomb, a hundred yards away was twisted metal that had been its tail unit. We ran to the houses and alerted the duty sentries who immediately evacuated the troops to the rear of the premises, a telephone call was passed to the authorities by an officer and sentries placed at barriers across the road. We left them to it and made our way back to our base.

We walked along the road and met a postman who was moving something in the road. When he saw us he called out "give us a hand mates". We hurried to him but stopped dead when we realised he was manhandling another very large German

bomb which he had already rolled from the entrance to a drive some twenty feet down the road.

He grumbled "These blasted soldiers have dropped something off their b****y lorry", then added "If I hadn't seen it I might have run into it with my bike and probably broken my arm or leg". When we enlightened to him as to the identity of the object, he ran off at such a speed, leaving his bicycle behind. He would have broken the four minute mile!

A total of six delayed action bombs had been dropped. We learned later that four were rendered safe by the Royal Engineers Bomb Disposal team and two exploded before the team arrived. One that exploded was the bomb moved by the 'four minute mile' postman and that went off about two hours after we were at the scene.

Little did I think that during all this excitement before too many years had passed I would be dealing, day after day, with explosive devices of all shapes and sizes. Strange world.

My Story Begins in 1942

Severe gales were raging in the North Sea, gigantic waves were breaking on our eastern coastline and much damage was done by hurricane force winds inland. Pitch black clouds raced across the midnight sky and clouds of spray rushed from the huge wave tops. Five miles off shore the waves were broken from below as the conning tower of a German U-Boat surfaced. As her hull came to the rough surface her diesel engines sprang into life. Her destination - the great Naval Port of Chatham.

I was standing behind the Captain with my finger on the trigger of a Very Light pistol, with every nerve straining. The bow and forestay halyards were causing sheets of spray and the waves were continuously breaking over the conning tower. Suddenly there was a shout from the lookout as dead ahead was a black shining object bobbing in the trough of a wave.

The Captain swiftly ordered a change of course and we veered away from the menacing object which, as it slid by, passed uncomfortably close to our port side hull to disappear into our wake. We could see it was a mine. I had seen my first mine and it was some time before my heart returned to normal!

The reason for the Very Light pistol was the British had captured an undamaged U-Boat and a British crew were taking it to Chatham for examination and conversion for use by the Royal Navy and didn't want to be shot up by "friends".

In those days people had a tendency to shoot first and ask question later so I was ready with the appropriate flares. I should have known from all this that for me the war years were to be packed with incidents. I was with submarines for a very short period and when I left was sent to HMS Vernon to learn more electrics.

Frogmen ?

Whilst I was an Ordinary Seaman at HMS Vernon, Portsmouth I was often on night sentry duty. Most times it was uneventful. On this occasion however it was anything but! Frequently there were rumours around a place like Vernon for it held Hitler's first secret weapon of destruction, which up to its discovery had caused thousands of tons of shipping to be sunk. The enemy at this time was not supposed to know that the secret had been discovered. The current rumour at this time was that enemy divers were visiting our ports, sinking ships and coming ashore silently killing anybody in sight, with knives. Sentries of course were prime targets.

On this night I was on the midnight watch and I was tired when I went on duty. It was one of those clammy nights with only a light warm breeze. The noises of a busy naval dockyard continued. From my patrol point near a jetty I saw two 'Hunt' class destroyers leaving harbour for action in the channel. They played over the ships tannoy, tunes such as "A hunting we will go" and other hunting songs.

All was quiet. My patrol took me to the rail head slip which sloped into the harbour water. The sea was quite choppy despite there being little wind. As I looked down into the water I noticed masses of flotsam consisting of floating timber and the odd box or two. Suddenly the surface was broken and a splash made it known that something or someone was causing this disturbance. I peered down 15 feet of the greasy wall to the water but my eyes could not detect the cause of the commotion. Managing to remain quite still, with my heart thumping and my knees beginning to shake, I watched.

There it was again, something was pushing the mass of floating rubbish aside. Then I saw the movement. The water was being parted in a line to the sloping slipway and the waters edge. Silently I placed the whistle, which sentries always had on lanyards round their necks, to my shaking lips. Now I could see a black shiny head poke through the rubbish, its eyes looked at me and it seemed to be wearing goggles. Quietly and slowly I moved back from the wall towards a large capstan. From there I looked directly down the slipway and could see the head moving slowly to the side away from the waters edge. Quietly I rammed a bullet into the breach and took off the safety catch on the rifle, then rested the barrel on the capstan top and was about to take aim when I heard a noise to my right from the direction of the buildings.

Turning I saw a Lieutenant RN approaching. I held up my hand hoping he would understand and approach quietly. He didn't so I called as softly as I could to say I thought there was a diver down below. "Bloody rubbish" he exploded. "Have you been drinking ?" and at the same time shone his bright light down to the water, the head remained motionless and quite suddenly came a few feet out of the water, turned and then sped away on the surface for several yards before submerging. "Its only a bloody seal, sailor" he said. "In future use your bloody sense", whereupon he stalked away.

My duty ended after another hour or so. I didn't mention my 'diver' to a soul. Why? Well before going on duty I did have an illicit tot of rum. Someone had a birthday and I had been invited to join them. I couldn't refuse a tot of rum from a chum, could I?

Early that evening I had been listening to a young sailor playing the piano to everyone's delight, he went on for hours. He was so good they wouldn't let him stop even for a rest. He played like Russ Conway but that was certainly not the name of this sailor, but then Russ Conway was a stage name and I cannot remember the name of the pianist, so who knows, it may have been Russ.

The Case of the Missing Hammock

My memory takes me back to the time when I was an ordinary seaman and the ship's company, which was resting at Westcliffe-on-Sea, was suddenly entrained late in the afternoon to set off to an unknown destination. By early morning the mountains of Scotland were in view and by late afternoon we detrained at Greenock where we assembled on the dockside. Three seaman plus myself were assigned as baggage party. Our job was to unload hammocks from the train onto trolleys and then wheel them to the dockside where they had to be correctly stacked awaiting the arrival of the MacBrayne steamer which was to take us to our still unknown destination.

After approximately two hours the steamer arrived and we (the baggage party) had to throw each hammock to the deck which was about three feet below the dockside wall. This task proved less than simple as the sea was rough causing the boat to yaw from time to time and at other times lying snug to the wall. It swung out by as much as ten feet, and it was at one such moment that a hammock which was thrown by one of the work party missed the deck and splashed some twenty feet down into the boiling scummy water.

The officer-in-charge dismissed any attempt to recover the errant hammock. We were prepared to have a go by borrowing a rowing boat moored nearby, but we were forbidden to try. After the Company had embarked on the ferry we chugged off to our mystery destination. By the time we arrived it was dark and the hammock party reformed to move the hammocks from the deck to stow them in the back of Royal Navy trucks.

When we arrived at the billet (which turned out to be a muddy peninsula covered in nissen huts at Rosneath) the petty officer in charge took each hammock and called out the name of the owner which was clearly printed on the side. The owner smartly collected his hammock and disappeared into the building, soon there were only twelve left and thirteen seamen waiting hopefully as the names were called out. At last all the hammocks were claimed and one seaman was left standing - me! It had been my hammock that had disappeared into the harbour at Greenock which meant I had to draw a new set from stores and although it was 11 pm (or 2300 hrs navy time) I had to get stencils and print on the new hammock my name and official number.

There is a sting in the tail of this tale. Pay day was in twelve days time. I received no pay and when I queried this I was told by the paymaster that the cost of the replacement hammock was deducted from my pay as I had lost the other one through negligence and that I was lucky not to be charged with losing His Majesty's stores!!! The temptation to desert was very strong at this point as I felt this to be a gross miscarriage of justice, but commonsense prevailed and I 'soldiered' on!

Shortly after this incident I was recommended for a commission.

Rosneath Combined Operations Group

Our LCT (Landing Craft Tank (MKV)) base was a muddy nissen hut camp mentioned in the previous chapter. It was spread over a large area. The jetty for the liberty boats and stores was about a quarter of a mile from the main base.

The hut I shared with part of my boat flotilla contained a mixed bunch of sailors and two leading seamen. Unfortunately we had to put up with three undisciplined Glasgow Gorbals thieves. Their manners were the worst, language incomprehensible with every other word "******". The base was also overrun with rats. At night extermination groups would go out to seek out the rats. Some were armed with heavy clubs, others carried torches.

One group would go to one side of a haystack in a nearby field and wack the side making lots of noise, the torch holders would illuminate the fleeing rats and the others would club to death as many as they could. But not so the Gorbals scum. They would lightly club the rats and, whilst they were groggy, cut off one or both of their back legs and laugh at these creatures attempting to escape. Most of us walked away in horror for no one dared to try to stop them.

Two days after the rat incident and after exercising all day in the Clyde, we returned to base. Most of the crews were given night leave ashore at Helensburgh and we were preparing to go to the first liberty boat. I went to my kit bag for my shaving gear and to my horror saw that the bottom had been cut out. I quickly discovered that my best suit had been taken. A few moments later one of the Gorbals scum appeared with my suit under his arm, he still wore his dirty working overalls.

I approached him quietly and asked what he was doing with my suit. He let out his usual curses and demanded to know what I was going to do about it. I grabbed for my suit but like greased lightening he produced a cut throat razor and whipped it a millimetre under my chin. Then he threw my suit in my face, turned and stormed out, telling all around that he 'would get me'. I was thoroughly demoralized and from that moment decided to desert. I was quite prepared to fight Fascists, Germans, Italians or Japanese, in fact that is why I joined the Navy, but certainly not the Scots!

My intention was not revealed to another soul. My plan was to go on my long weekend leave which was due in two days, not to return from that leave but desert and join the RAF. Making several visits to the canteen I managed to obtain a supply of biscuits and extra cigarettes.

The day of the weekend leave was uneventful. I had left my LCT clean and shipshape, packed my small case fully and had several meals in the canteen. I was ready and waiting for the tannoy to announce 'Liberty men ashore'. It came as I was halfway through my second cup of tea which I slowly finished, popped into the loo and then made my way down to the jetty. With several others I was almost to the jetty when the Liberty boat left, and the next boat was not due for another hour so I took myself back to the warm canteen.

I had just ordered a cup of tea when the tannoy spat out a clear instruction, "Able Seaman Cashford to report immediately to the Duty Staff Officer". My knees started knocking. How could anyone know that I was about to desert? I decided to brave a meeting and duly presented myself. The Duty Officer was a nice guy and lucky for me he was my flotilla RNVR Lieutenant, therefore he knew me.

My knees were still knocking, but what he told me was that I had been recommended for a commission and that I must proceed to Portsmouth that night for a preliminary selection board. My reaction was "But Sir, I can't afford to be an officer". He soon enlightened me. Stating that before the Navy he was a mortuary assistant with no funds when he commissioned. He put me at ease and asked what I had been going to do on my lost weekend leave. I told him everything including, in desperation, why I was going to desert and then join the RAF.

He was totally sympathetic but reminded me that if I turned down the Selection Board offer I would have to stay with Combined Operations. He added "If you fail the Board you will be posted elsewhere". I thanked him, went to my hut and prepared to leave. Four hours later I was on my way to Portsmouth. Two days later I passed the selection board and was accepted as an officer cadet. Once again I was sent on indefinite leave, a very much happier person.

Three days into my 'indefinite' leave a friendly policeman arrived at my Mother's house with instructions for me to report to Portsmouth. Once there I was posted, on a temporary basis, to a Naval unit at Calshot, more of which in the next chapter.

Adventure at Calshot Spit

Not long after the "trip" on the U Boat and seeing my first live mine I was recommended for a commission. There was a waiting time for a place at the Officer Training School and to fill in this time they sent me to Calshot near Southampton. The job turned out to be a young sailor's dream. It was delivering "By Hand Only" documents to the flying boat base at Calshot Spit, a cycling distance of about two miles. Now the Navy, like the other services did not seem able to supply the correct sized equipment for its personnel. The bicycle issued to me was the largest framed machine in the pool and I stand 5'6"! Requests for a change were ignored but I did manage to make several uneventful trips. Then I met my "Waterloo" ......

The morning was most pleasant, hardly any clouds in the sky, with my "Hands of Officer Only" packages firmly secured I mounted my mighty steed and set off - it felt good to be alive. Below me the sea was very blue and several craft were plying between the Isle of Wight and the mainland. Three destroyers were making passage to their moorings at Southampton.

Coming toward me I observed a bearded Commander also mounted on a bicycle, one more fitted to his size than mine was to me. The gold braid on his sleeves glittered in the sunshine. Suddenly all hell broke loose. Streaking across the water not more than a hundred feet up came two German fighters. They proceeded to bomb and machine gun the small craft on the water and I thought I saw some direct hits. One of the fighters turned and came toward me firing his cannon as he came. Lumps of asphalt were hurled upwards and I threw myself off my bike into the weeds on my left. In seconds it was over, the planes disappeared as quickly as they came and the only sound was of occasional anti aircraft fire. On the water one ship seemed to be making smoke but otherwise everything looked as it had before.

Picking myself up and checking to make sure I was still in one piece I recovered my bike which fortunately was undamaged so I prepared to re mount. By now the officer who had been riding toward me drew level and proceeded to give me the biggest dressing down I had ever had. Why? - because I had failed to salute him! We British are undoubtedly a peculiar race. Not a word was said about the incidents which had just taken place, the visit from the Luftwaffe and the cannon fire throwing lumps of asphalt all over the place. Still it takes all sorts, doesn't it?

13

Officer Training School

After my stint at Calshot I was once again sent on indefinite leave. Everyone said I would be at home for at least six weeks before recall. After just three days the police again came to the house with instructions for me to report the following morning to HMS King Alfred, Hove, Sussex. From there it was on to the Officers Training College which had been a girl's school before the war and was situated at Lancing which turned out to be rather vulnerable to 'incidents'.

On one occasion the entire assembly of cadets were square bashing (marching to the uninitiated) on the grass in front of the school. It was a beautiful day with the sun shining all the morning. There must have been at least five hundred cadets drilling when, without warning, two Messerschmitt 109 fighter/bombers skimmed over the surrounding roof tops. What a target we presented. With cannons firing they blasted away for what seemed minutes but could have been only seconds. We dispersed in all directions. I and my immediate companions rushed for some cover by some outbuildings and before the fighters came back were crouched behind solid brick walls. Back they screamed with machine guns firing continuously and shell cases spraying all over the place.

Just as suddenly as they appeared, they were gone and we stood up feeling decidedly foolish as we realized we had taken shelter behind a glass house. As we were standing there we heard a bomb explode somewhere near. It turned out to be a direct hit on the Shoreham gasometer which promptly burst into flames. The other fighter successfully bombed the Brighton Viaduct. The extraordinary thing was not one soul was injured in the incident except for one chap who fell on the grass and broke either his leg or arm whilst running for cover.

I passed training with good marks, received my nice new uniform as a Temporary Acting Sub Lieutenant RNVR and was sent to the Naval College at Greenwich for appointment.

AA HQ Fanum House, The Aldwych, London

I am always being asked how I became a Bomb & Mine Disposal Officer. This is how! At Greenwich College their Lordships discovered that my eyesight would prevent me from being a watchkeeper or take charge of a ship at sea. I therefore would have to find a more suitable appointment. With David B, another Sub Lieutenant with poor eyesight, we were given four options.

(1) Censor Officer. I just couldn't see myself reading and blue penciling other peoples love letters.

(2) Passive Defence Officer. No thank you. I couldn't see myself as a sea going ARP Warden. (Air Raid Precaution).

(3) Courier (sometimes in civilian clothes). Maybe I had read too many Istanbul Express type novels where couriers receive a knife in the back. This was not for me.

(4) Special Duties Officer. By now I had no options left so plumped for this without knowing what it entailed.

Both David B and I were accepted. After spending several nights during air raids fire watching over the college's beautiful painted hall, we were given two special identity cards and instructed to go to the Automobile Association HQ at Fanum House, The Aldwych, London.

We arrived and were scrutinised by the first security guard. We went through the sand bagged entrance hall to the second check. Five minutes later my name was called and I was greeted by a commander who curtly ordered me to 'follow him'. We proceeded through a doorway into a large darkened room, the only light came from the far off open doorway. As I followed I was aware that six or seven coffin like shaped objects, covered with white sheets, lay on the floor to my left. My mind began to play tricks, what had I let myself in for?

I didn't have time to speculate for we soon got through the dark room and the open door and there stood a full Captain RN. The Commander announced me as Cashford, the Captain grabbed me by the hand and said, "Well done Cashford, you are now one of a band of elite officers in my Bomb and Mine Disposal Department".

I was, to use a modern phrase, gob smacked. He then told me they were going to train me to render safe bombs, parachute mines, sea mines and any other unexploded objects. "Not only that" he said, "We shall also train you to render safe under water." With that I was dismissed and returned to Greenwich College, David B followed shortly afterwards.

I spent another week at Greenwich College, mainly on fire watching at night on the roof. It was during this period that I took a short cut through the underground passages of the building, to avoid heavy rain, that I saw the ghost of an Elizabethan lady. I had not been drinking and it was in the morning, but that's another story. After this I received my joining instructions to proceed forthwith to HMS Volcano, somewhere in Cumberland.

I eventually discovered what those coffin shaped objects were. They were previously rendered safe parachute mines and were used as practice items for us budding Bomb and Mine Disposal Officers!

Journey Into a Strange New World

The train was full (including the corridor). At 7.32 pm it slowly pulled out of King's Cross. It was already dark. Just beyond the station approaches we came to an abrupt halt. Cases and parcels fell from the racks onto the unsuspecting passengers. Thankfully, no-one was hurt and we quickly got everything sorted out and stowed away again. Trains moved slowly beside us and for some moments there was silence then a guards officer got up and opened the window. Smoke and soot from outside mixed with the smoke of the overcrowded carriage. We came to realise there were many bombers overhead and sticks of bombs dropped nearby. An enormous bang came from somewhere near the engine and I began to wonder if I would ever get to Drigg!

Despite all the mayhem about us there was a surprising calmness amongst the others in the carriage so I dare not show my fear. Several more explosions occurred nearby and, as there was nothing we could do about it, we shared our cigarettes and made small talk. An hour passed during which there were only occasional explosions. Some buildings nearby had suffered direct hits and huge fires blazed through them which the firemen were fighting to control.

When the train suddenly jerked into motion there were cheers from all directions. It slowly gathered speed. Little could be seen owing to the dense smoke from hundreds of fires raging on each side of the track. Another cheer rang out when an aircraft was seen to fall in flames. I did not join the cheering as I wondered if it could have been one of our night fighters and not an enemy plane.

The train continued north through the darkened countryside. The passengers could now eat the food that had lovingly been prepared by wives and mothers from their all too meagre rations. After eating we slept and when I awoke it was almost daybreak. A beautiful sunrise lit the east making it hard to believe the carnage we had seen the night before.

An hour or two later the train chugged into Barrow in Furness and all passengers disembarked. The platform was full of Air Force personnel, officers and sergeants displaying the wings of aircrew and there wasn't an unhappy face amongst them and my spirits rose with them. I picked up my Admiralty pattern suitcase (Officer's for the use of) and went to the canteen which was operated by the ladies from the W.V.S. who were working like beavers in their effort to meet the needs of hungry and thirsty souls. Wondering why I seemed to be creating a lot of interest I realised there were no other Naval types about, just every other branch of the services!

Two hours later, the train to Ravenglass (the station for Drigg) came puffing into the station and then having climbed aboard we were on our way. From the train I could see several airfields, two of which had barrage balloons on the perimeter, also some Wellington bombers were taking off or landing.

Arriving at Ravenglass I stepped onto the platform. A short chubby Leading Wren Rating came across, saluted and enquired if I was Sub Lieutenant Cashford. It was nice to know they were expecting me. I was quite impressed and followed my guide out of the station to a truck. My case was stowed in the back and we proceeded to my new base.

Before leaving London it had been impressed upon me that I was going to a **MOST SECRET** establishment so imagine my surprise and amusement when the truck arrived at the entrance to a large house and there for all the world to see was an Admiralty type sign-board proclaiming **"H.M.S. VOLCANO"**. What an extraordinary name to give to a "secret" establishment which was to teach the art of rendering safe all types of unexploded bombs, mines and other devices designed to kill or maim.

It was at this "most secret" establishment we were instructed in the use of explosives both on land and underwater. After an extensive course which occupied several days, we had to lay underwater charges in the fast flowing river that bordered the grounds. These small demolition charges were to be exploded by electrical dyno-charger and we were highly suspicious as to why we were not allowed to test our handiwork. Every day different groups had to lay charges but were never privileged to see what happened when the plunger was plunged!

Upon returning to the river one day a group found their handiwork had been exploded and only pieces of electrical cable remained. We had a little conference and all were determined to solve this mystery. It was a few days later that all was revealed. It seems that someone in authority was, under cover of darkness, blowing the charges and reaping a rich harvest! The sting in the tail; we were served tinned salmon in the mess, never fresh. Visiting the local inn we overheard the landlord and the water bailiff discussing concern felt for the large number of stunned but uninjured fish found 'below that secret place on the hill' and also heard that poachers were being sought and that the local police were alerted to the 'funny goings on'. Ten of us who joined 'Volcano' on the same day held a council of war and resolved to teach the culprit or culprits a lesson. Of one thing we were sure: the officer instructors at Volcano were not involved in any way.

Our next assignment was to lay charges in the river and we set about our task with unusual enthusiasm. It was an uncomfortable job to say the least. The six charges, small sticks of Polar Blasting Gelignite (PBG) were placed across the river at depths around five to six feet in the muddy water, detonators were fitted and electrical joints adequately insulated with tape and made waterproof by coating with a gluey shellac like material known as Canadian balsam. The cable from each charge was then led to a riverside firing point, the ends insulated and secured to a small red post. We had done our job very well and knew it would be inspected later. What wasn't easily noticed was that one charge had been placed very near to the river bank below the firing post. The water at this point was at least six feet deep, a very suitable location.

During dinner that night several dull thumps were heard. We stole discreet looks at one another and the senior Wren Officer voiced the opinion it was thunder from the Eskdale area. We said nothing. One strange outcome of this little exercise was fresh salmon appeared on the menu in the mess quite often. After a time we heard about the events of that particular night and of the involuntary swim by an unknown gentleman.

Because of his concern, the water bailiff had hidden in thick cover on the opposite bank. He noticed the red post but could not imagine its purpose. It was almost dark when he saw movement and watched as someone, obviously in uniform, quietly moved to the post and fumbled with something for several minutes. Then a series of dull thumps occurred on the river bed and small columns of water rose a few feet from the surface and splashed down. The bank under the figure disintegrated in a large plume of water and he slipped gracefully into the river. Surfacing, he swam lower down stream. Joe, the water watcher, would not say who the swimmer was. Maybe he didn't know but we did notice one hat peg reserved for senior officers was empty for several days. Then it sported a brand new hat! As you can imagine this was a great topic for discussion in the local pub.

My six weeks training was almost over and I knew my nerves wouldn't stand much more for we ended the course by learning how to deal with booby traps and you never knew where they were likely to "pop" up.

Going to the bathroom became particularly nerve wracking, even picking up your shoes could bring a 'pop', opening doors, etc. It made you very cautious to say the least. The following story illustrates how booby traps could affect lives!!

Boobies

The instructors at Volcano were extremely good, all quite outstanding persons in their way. Maybe some were a little more eccentric than others but even so they considered they had failed in their task if any of the course was killed whilst working on unexploded devices!

The drill was that one party laid booby traps and another party had to locate them and render them safe. We all got extremely cunning at this and even when the day's work was over you could not relax. Pick up a shoe - BANG! Flush the toilet - BANG! Lie on the bed - BANG! They even used delayed action charges so that you could open a suitcase or a drawer and nothing would happen so you relaxed then, unexpectedly - BANG! Our instructors encouraged this activity so within the week although the booby traps were laid in increasing numbers practically all were rendered safe.

One way they made us very cautious was your name would be put on the 'DECEASED' board if you exploded a booby trap. That concentrated the mind wonderfully. It was during one of the 'booby' periods that an incident occurred which I'm certain will never be forgotten by two people.

A heavy practice day had passed and after dinner three of us toddled down to the local inn because we knew a consignment of beer had been delivered. After an enjoyable evening it was quite late by the time we reached HMS Volcano again. We passed through the gate with its **"Keep out - Military only"** notice and walked toward the house along the winding tree darkened drive. We were chatting away when John remembered his party had laid a really cunning booby trap among the trees "Who cleared it?" he enquired. As I was in the other party I was able to state we had not found it. We decided to see if we could find it then and render it safe.

We stepped off the drive in the general direction of our target which we estimated lay about 100 yards away when there was a violent bang some twenty feet away followed by another and then a bright flash from a small flare. A scream filled the air and through the glare two partly clothed bodies (one definitely female) rushed away toward the main gate. We collected the items of discarded clothing and took them to the main gate where we hoped the 'victims' may be hiding in the bushes. We discussed in loud voices where we were putting the clothes.

Returning to the house we went into the mess and sweet talked the duty wren into serving us each a drink and one for herself. After half an hour we tossed a coin to see which one should go to the gate to see if the clothes had been collected. I lost! When I got there no clothes remained but where we had left them was a piece of paper on which was printed in bold letters THANKS and on the other side FOR NOTHING. I bet those two always remember HMS Volcano!!

The Day I Saw a Submarine

At HMS Volcano there were two large motor launches that were used for practicing mine location and recovery in the shallow waters of Ravenglass harbour. One launch was rather 'sick' so it was to be taken along the coast to the shipyard at Whitehaven for engine and hull repairs and I was assigned to the faulty launch which was to be escorted by its sister launch. The day was fine but a very heavy sea was running and our escort soon got fed-up with our slow speed and high tailed it around Bees Head to her destination leaving us to wallow along.

Our skipper was far from happy having had an early morning drinking session at the local hostelry and we were hardly making any headway against the strengthening wind and tide. As I have mentioned before I'm a rotten sailor and before long seasickness overtook me. Hanging over the rail in approved fashion I came up for air for the umpteenth time when, about a quarter of a mile or less on our port beam, I saw what appeared to be a periscope pop up, do a 'watch' then down. It had been reported by the coastguard a few days earlier that a submarine was spotted on the surface at dawn. This fact floated into my memory.

Feeling terrible I staggered to the wheelhouse but the senior officer didn't want to know, therefore I returned to the rail where, within ten minutes, up pops the periscope, this time less than twenty feet ahead of us. Of course it was a periscope, hadn't I been in submarines long enough to know? The engine of the launch seemed to be coughing more than ever and with my eyes glued to the roughening waves where the periscope had been I resolved that under no circumstances would I be taken prisoner by a U-Boat. Deciding there and then to jump overboard as soon as the sub surfaced and swim to the shore.

Suddenly, there it was, not a foot from the side of our launch. It seemed as though the U-Boat skipper was going to surface and lift the launch out of the water. Getting ready to jump I watched mesmerised as the periscope slid along the side of the launch and as it came level I grabbed it. Goodness knows why for I was lifted off the deck and it was at that moment that my seasickness left me. In seconds it was apparent that I had blundered and felt the biggest twit in the Navy, for my periscope turned out to be a broken but heavy wooden spar, probably from a cargo ship sunk in the Atlantic and it

had drifted into the Irish Sea. It had some lamp units built into it and was possibly twenty feet long with its heavy end down in the depths. Maybe there were cables attached which caused its motion to be slow and dip down under the waves.

By now the wind had increased to almost gale force and fortunately the other crew members were being very seasick during this incident and therefore were unable to bear witness to my stupidity!   We arrived at Whitehaven not much the worse for our experience and our skipper was almost sober by landfall.

By the Book

When training finished I spent rather boring weeks waiting to 'do' my first job of rendering safe. Each day during this period was occupied with swotting up the relatively few written instructions issued by the Admiralty and tools got checked daily! Then a panic signal was received, just when I had begun to think nobody knew where I was and had forgotten me. A mine had washed ashore on the island of Tiree which was one of a series of small islands spread off the west coast of Scotland which of course necessitated a flight, my first. It must seem strange to younger people today that I was twenty years old before I went up in an aeroplane, but of course there were not the opportunities in those days.

This was a PRIORITY TASK, for Tiree was very important to the RAF as it contained an airfield on which pilots converted from flying twin-engined aircraft to much larger four-engined ones. Each aircraft took off and flew westward into the Atlantic. After a few hours they turned 180° and made landfall with the aid of a radio beam. It was therefore vital that the radio masts were not damaged by exploding mines.

So, at last, I was assigned my first 'job'. With some feeling of relief I learned I would go in the company of Sub Lieutenant W, who was already pretty experienced having been active in bomb & mine disposal for some 6 months or so. We met for the first time at Renfrew RAF station. He was pure Liverpudlian and a good bit older with plenty of grey hair making this clear. We liked each other on sight.

The weather was, as usual, dreadful with gales blowing and torrential rain, the reason no doubt the mine had come ashore. We ran through the heavy rain across a grass runway to a twin-engined bi-plane which was standing in three inches of water. I was not excited, just scared stiff! After we were seated in the plane, first one and then the other engine spluttered into life and gradually increased in power, driving sheets of rain and mist passed the windows. We moved off and seemed to be heading at great speed along the saturated grass straight toward a gigantic hanger. At this moment I shut my eyes, and waited for what I thought was the inevitable crash when, with a huge roar the aircraft left the ground and rose rapidly into the air. As I opened my eyes I saw the roof of the hanger disappearing a few feet below us then the aircraft turned on its side quite violently and the radio operator (who must have had very strong arms) was holding the radio on its shelf.

When we levelled out I saw to my horror that we were flying parallel to the barrage balloons which flew over and around the airfield and Port Glasgow, so before even seeing the sea I was a nervous wreck. My colleague (tutor) was reading a paperback quite unconcerned. Touchdown was exciting but uneventful. The aircraft, which was a De Havilland Dominée, taxied to its parking spot. Upon stepping onto the tarmac we were greeted by some RAF types, a Flight Lt and a pretty WAAF driver who took us to the coastguard who had sighted the mine in a sandy bay.

Having been deposited near the site of the mine, we hauled our respective tool bags across great boulders for about a quarter of a mile to the bay which was about the length of two cricket pitches, some twenty feet from the rocks and to where the sea was breaking on the shore. Close to where we were standing lay a British Mark 17 mine and it looked in good condition with black paintwork which looked polished! To our astonishment at the other end of the bay was its twin. We hadn't one 'job' but two.

Sub Lt W, being my tutor, directed me to deal with the mine nearest and he elected to go to the other. I knew exactly what to do. Remember I had spent days pouring over the manuals whilst waiting for the 'call'. Away I went, checked the base plate - it was OK, and after removing the detonator cap I put my hand through the 3" hole felt the detonator terminals carefully. Releasing first one and then the other cable, I pulled them away from the detonator terminals and my mine was now almost safe. I had a short rest then took two felt lined wooden boxes from my tool bag. These were to safely transport the dangerous detonator and booster. Having carefully removed the said detonator I laid it in its felt lined box and closed the lid and repeated the operation with the booster. Now 6 cwt of TNT was harmless.

Sometimes the terrain is unsuitable for vehicles to get close enough to recover mines for disposal so they have to be dismantled on site and the explosive destroyed. This is done by burning. This being such an occasion I started to prepare for demolition. Looking along the bay it seemed that Sub Lt W. was at about the same stage as myself. Removing all nuts and bolts from the top and bottom plates allowed the wind, which was whistling along the sand, to blow right through the mine which was as the text books advised. When ignited the wind would then blow the intense heat, smoke and flames away from the mine and toward the sea; the mine was conveniently lying in the right position. Placing paraffin soaked waste inside the cavity, after several attempts it ignited and my fire started.

Quoting from the manual (required reading for all disposal officers) it read in large print, "IF THE FLAMES REDUCE AND IT IS REPLACED BY ABNORMAL AMOUNTS OF SMOKE THE AREA MUST BE IMMEDIATELY EVACUATED AS THERE IS SUBSTANTIAL RISK OF AN EXPLOSION". My smoke was as it should be and the wind was obligingly sending it toward the Atlantic. Packing my tools I placed the bag on a rock near our exit path. It was then I looked toward Sub Lt W. to see how he was progressing. His fire was also lit, mine was about halfway through with the flames shooting out about ten or so feet but his fire had almost stopped then black blobs of smoke were issuing forth (just like an Indian smoke signal). Something had definitely gone wrong.

I shouted to him but the wind blew my call back to me so I started to run toward him continuing to shout. He was standing beside the mine when suddenly there was a bright flash, and I was blown onto my back landing in the loose sand. How long I lay there is impossible to tell but when I gathered my wits the sky was blotted out by tons of wet sand, stones and pieces of metal so I could not have been there very long. Getting shakily to my feet I attempted to brush sand from my face, hair and clothes. I also recovered my cap which had fallen nearby, then I stood rooted to the spot as hot metal continued to fall into the sea making sizzling noises and leaving steam on the surface.

Behind me my fire was still burning brightly and all I could hear was a high pitched whistle. Staggering across the sand to where I had last seen my colleague there was a crater some twenty feet across already filled with water but of my colleague - not a sign. Standing frozen to the spot, spitting sand from my mouth I seemed unable to think but at last managed to look around and facing the rocks saw a movement. Running over I could see something that looked like bits of a naval uniform covered in sand. Minutes later the sand was cleared away and shortly after that Sub Lt W. was sitting on a rock totally unhurt, no cuts, bruises or scratches but when he began to talk and I could hear again, didn't he stutter!

Why did the mine explode? There are several reasons why this could have occurred, such as omitting to remove the top or base plates properly thus preventing the fire being blown away from the mine. The detonator was in its box but I do not remember seeing the booster although the box was there. Who knows? Whatever the reason it could have been fatal.

It must have been a year or so after this that I heard he had died during a flu epidemic, which seemed terribly sad having survived the mine incident.

Demolished!

Walking to my office I met my chief who was on his way to see me and it was, as usual, raining. He informed me that there was a demolition job for me to do at an Air Force base on the north west coast of Scotland and that an aircraft was waiting for me at Renfrew. He couldn't, or wouldn't, tell me more so gathering my tools and some explosives and travelling in a naval vehicle sporting red flags, we left for the airfield at Renfrew.

Waiting on the grass runway was a Dominée, a twin engined biplane similar to the peace time version used mainly for inter-island flights. The engines were warming up and, in the still pouring rain, I climbed aboard. With the engines racing we moved across the grass for take off. We splashed through wide puddles and the engine seemed to falter, then we crawled our way upwards, flying too close for my comfort to the barrage balloons around the west of Glasgow.

Suddenly the engines misfired and thankfully we returned to the airfield, myself with my heart in my mouth. We landed and I had to leave the Dominée to wait in a very cold hut for some fitters to work on the faulty engines.

Two hours later we set off once more, and this time scraped between two balloons before flying toward a very high brick chimney which we hopped over. I was extremely unhappy and came to the conclusion that rendering safe mines and bombs was a much safer occupation!

We eventually landed and as we ran along the tarmac I noticed that everyone wore a gas mask. Just my luck I thought to arrive as some zealous Gas Officer has decided to have gas drill. I reached for my gas mask and realised in horror that I hadn't got it with me. When I was in the very cold hut at Renfrew I had it then, but I certainly hadn't got it now. This was a very serious and punishable offence anyway, so I was more than worried! We talked to the Control Tower and could see, through the windows, that all the crew there were wearing gas masks.

As our plane came to a halt and the engines stopped an officer, also wearing a gas mask, came down the Control Tower steps. Collecting my gear and buttoning my Burberry up to the neck I jumped down to the tarmac. The officer beckoned me to follow him. It was only when we had walked away from the smell of the aviation fuel near the plane that the awful stench was apparent. I thought the Gas Officer had really gone over the top, introducing stink bombs for more realism. Coughing and spluttering and wishing for a cigarette I followed the Flight Lt. to a 15 cwt pick-up truck where he indicated by pointing, that I should climb aboard.

Still refusing to remove his gas mask he used sign language of sorts but I didn't understand what he was trying to convey. He drove to the end of the runway, past dispersal to the very end of the tarmac where he stopped and indicated that I should go up a high sand bank covered with marram grass. Leaving my raincoat behind; (thankfully it had stopped raining), I gathered my tools and explosives and set off with the smell increasing in density with every step. At the top of the bank I saw the sea and there, about 50 yards away, was the source of the stench, a very large and very dead whale and I realised this called for some very swift action on my part.

I did my calculations and decided on a plan. Quickly I made up three bundles of demolition charges and as the tide had turned and was beginning to flow again I donned my seaboots. With the spade from the truck and the charges I had prepared I set off down the foreshore across some wet mud into about 36 inches of water around the dead hulk.

With difficulty I climbed to the highest part of the head and with the spade dug through the putrid flesh to excavate a hole for my first charge. Climbing and slithering to the middle of the carcass, the drill was repeated, then to the final position three quarters along the hulk. On this particular day I made three mistakes; the first one was to forget my gas mask (and couldn't I have done with it). The second came shortly after I had lit the fuses. Having placed all the slow burning (one foot per minute) fuses in their TNT charges I moved from the head of the beast and threw the spade up onto the sand bank. No one was near as I had made certain that the Flight Lt. had arranged for himself and anyone else not to be within a quarter of a mile radius (just in case things went wrong). I searched inland and out to sea - nothing moved so I bent down to light the nearest fuse and hurried as best I could to the other two. These were also ignited and that was when the second mistake occurred for I jumped off the

hulk and promptly dropped into six feet of water as I had been too busy to notice that the tide was coming in very fast, I waded out of the water as swiftly as I could but as I reached the edge all three charges detonated.

Great lumps of blubber hit me in the back and knocked me down and I ended up in the sea again and that's when I noticed the third mistake. With the tide, I had failed to

notice that the off sea wind had freshened and it picked up the great mass of stinking parts of whale, taking it 300 or so feet into the sky then deposited it gently throughout the airfield parade ground, the hangers and other buildings.

I'm afraid I was less than popular and they flew me back to Renfrew quickly, I'm sure for my own safety! Even the aircrew glared at me but that may have been because I did not smell all that sweet. Even after my clothes were washed the 'perfume' hung for a long time and the smell remained in my odour retaining senses for many years after the incident.

Lady Luck Rock - Island of Tiree

Leaning into the gale force wind with squalls of rain lashing into my face I walked to the rocky bay where, the coastguard said, the big black mine lay. He also warned me that the tide was rising and the mine would be awash within forty minutes or so. I hurried as fast as I could across wet rocks and about twenty feet down a rock face to a beach where forty yards to seaward was a large pinnacle of black rock below which was a British Mark 17 Contact Mine. The sea rushed in from the Atlantic, and great rollers twenty to thirty feet high dashed against the rocks further out to sea, making a fantastic din.

I worked as quickly as I could, although having great difficulty removing the bung to the detonator housing as on its journey across the rocks and beach the mine had been damaged and this had distorted the bung threads, but eventually it was removed. By this time the occasional wave broke just behind my rock and the broken water rushed toward me and around my feet, reminding me that time was running out. Groping inside the mine shell through the 4" hole I located the detonator head and with fingers which were well practised disconnected the wire from one terminal and then the other. The cable was carefully pulled through the bung hole. Once free insulation tape was applied and then the wires put back. The detonator was gripped firmly and lifted gently out of its housing. Another wave broke sending thunderous noise across the rocks as the water ran up the beach and was now over my knees. When it receded the suction was enormous.

The detonator was now out of the mine and my next task required great care as I had to dismantle the detonator housing and place the detonator in a prepared, insulated carrier box to protect it from any knocks. With the detonator in my fingers I was opening the special box when another huge wave broke beyond the rock. Suddenly the sky was illuminated followed by a gigantic explosion, for seconds I was both blinded and deafened and then I was aware of huge pieces of metal and rock falling around me. I crouched down terrified but nothing hit me, then there was silence. Another wave broke sending water up the beach now almost up to my thighs and cold sea water filled my wellies. As it rushed up the beach, it washed over red hot metal which sizzled like frying bacon.

I gathered my bits and pieces from the mine, picked up my wet tool bag and hurried up the beach where I saw, on drying sand, a large chunk of hot metal which I recognised as the base plate of a German 'Y' Contact mine which, unnoticed, had washed ashore to detonate on the seaward side of my sheltering rock.

At the RAF Officers Mess just before going to bed, pleasantly full of best scotch whisky, I noticed a map of the Island hanging on the wall and when I examined it I noticed that the name of the rock at the base of which the rogue mine had detonated was. LADY LUCK ROCK. I slept well that night. Someone was surely watching over me!

Flying Again with the R.A.F

The usual gale was blowing with great ferocity when a messenger came to tell me a mine had been washed ashore on the west coast of Tiree, an area of high priority. With the usual great haste I collected my tools and boarded the pool truck which had been summoned and we raced through the early morning darkness to Renfrew aerodrome just outside Glasgow arriving there at 07.20. Once again it was raining damned hard and the wind blew unhindered across the grass runways and between the nissen hut offices and hangers.

After about an hour waiting I was taken by pick-up truck to where a very wet twin-engined biplane stood. I met the pilot, who was extremely young looking even to me and I was only twenty. I was ushered into the cabin which contained seats for six or seven souls, choosing a seat near the wing which also gave me a good view of the engine and its propeller (I was still not a seasoned aircraft passenger). Ahead sat the pilot and to his rear left crouched an airman who was obviously the radio operator as he was fiddling with coils and earphones, adjusting this and that.

The wind had reduced somewhat but there were still gusts which rocked the aircraft violently and my nervous system was having a 'ball'. I was almost sick with a combination of fear and the overpowering smell of aviation spirit. After a while the door was shut and a crackle came from the radio, the starboard engine was started and, after what seemed an eternity, the port engine which promptly coughed and died.

Mechanics worked in the rain for ten minutes and the smell of the fuel nearly finished me but then the port engine restarted and within seconds both engines roared and the aircraft turned forty five degrees to starboard. Ahead as far as visibility would allow, was an expanse of wet grass.

The engine noise rose to a scream and we were bumping along at a fair speed passing through great puddles which sent sheets of water cascading over the engine and against the window, faster and faster we went when suddenly I was pushed back in my hard seat as we became airborne. A sigh of relief was short lived for ahead of us were the dreaded barrage balloons flying at different heights above and below us.

The pilot looked worried I thought and he certainly seemed to be grappling with the controls, the engine note changed and we lifted upwards and eventually over the nearest balloon and entered thick cloud. Good I thought, now I won't see one if it is in the way! Soon we were above the cloud and ahead was the brown and purple of a mountainside.

The radio operator moved over to the pilot and spoke to him after which he came to me with a message on a piece of paper (the noise in that plane made speech impossible) on which was written "Do you want some excitement? We will help you find some b***** mines". What could I do? I couldn't lose face to the RAF so nodded in agreement and away went the messenger.

Soon the radio was manned again and I was relaxing a little and gazing out of my window thinking that flying was not so bad after all when suddenly the starboard wing lifted and for a while I looked at the top of a mountain, then came a falling feeling and my stomach came into my mouth and my fingers gripped the seat in front so hard I'm sure they dug through the upholstery.

After falling what seemed hundreds of feet I saw, a mere twenty feet or so below, mountain sheep scattering in all directions as though from the devil himself and a few seconds later the shepherd dropped on his face as the aircraft swept over him. I swear to this day that the wing tips were not more than twenty to forty feet from the steep mountainside.

In a while we flattened out and looking past the pilot I could see we were approaching a vee shaped opening in the mountains. I didn't think there was enough space for us to get through so I shut my eyes..... When I opened them we were through! Below the mountain sloped down to a basin. To the left could be seen yellow sand and the sea and ahead the red blotch of a large coastal town.

The pilot followed the land contour and shortly came to the edge of the town, skimming over the church tower and roof tops with only feet to spare. There, for a second, was the railway station. A train was about to leave and great puffs of smoke rushed upwards and we flew right through it. I'm sure we were only about six feet above the highest points and I was damned scared. We skimmed across the sand and headed toward the open sea climbing to about 600 feet where I was fascinated by the different shades of green in the sea breaking around rocks which were peeping through the cold stormy water. We continued and, later on, flew over some larger rocks. For the first time in my life I saw seals which were diving into the water obviously frightened by this noisy bird disturbing their rest.

Presently the radio operator indicated with his thumb that we were going down which I took to mean we had arrived at Tiree for which I was truly thankful. My relief was short lived, however, as we certainly went down - in a dive. My tool bag left my feet and rushed toward the radio operator then its journey was checked as we flattened out with an accompanying roar from the engines. Now we flew at wave-top height as the crew were searching each rocky island for any mines that could have been washed ashore. Fortunately they soon got fed-up with looking, the switchback ended and we gained height.

Passing below us through the rough water we could see the unmistakable shape of a submarine cruising under the surface, its periscope breaking the surface once or twice. The radio operator was busy with his equipment reporting the sighting, and on we flew. I never did hear whether it was one of ours or one of theirs.

When we landed and I went to render safe the mine it turned out to be a harmless smoke float! The return trip must have been uneventful for I do not remember much about it. Thankfully from my point of view I think the pilot and his radio operator had all their excitement on the journey out and just wanted to get back to base!

Incident at Ardrossan

On an autumn afternoon I was instructed to proceed to Ardrossan as the police had reported that a fisherman had found a large mine at the ebbing of the tide. Gathering my tools I loaded them into the truck that had called for me. As I had the luxury of a driver I was able to swot up on my mine identity booklets.

Eventually we arrived at the scene to find the police had cordoned off a large area of the sand and foreshore and all windows of premises on the coast road were open, just in case of an explosion. Walking across the sands I came to the 'object' which lay in a shallow depression surrounded by a few inches of water. I had never seen, read or heard of anything remotely like this 'thing'. It was some fifteen feet long and three feet in diameter, fitted with rails on each side and had two suspension rings on the upper side. Each end was domed and through the centre from end to end was a tube some 1½ inches diameter from one end of which there appeared to be a movable lever which was coated in thick grease. All efforts to identify the object failed. Nothing in the booklets gave any hints.

Dusk was falling and the tide was coming in so, borrowing strong ropes and steel cable from the fishermen ashore, I firmly secured the object. By this time the tide had risen above my knees so I hurried up to the coast road. Efforts to contact my boss failed and I had to explain the position to the police and stayed enjoying their hospitality until the oncoming tide had covered the object with several feet of water. It didn't explode!

It was 22.00 hours (10 pm.) before I managed to make telephone contact with my boss whereupon he instructed me to return to Greenock and then go back to Ardrossan when the tide was low. In the meantime he would contact HMS Vernon at Portsmouth to see what they could come up with. Leaving Ardrossan we headed northwards on the coast road. As always it was raining heavily and rounding a bend in the road I could see someone in uniform attempting to thumb a lift. I asked the driver to stop and give the airman a lift. Once settled in the truck he explained that they had a 'flap' on and because of this he had missed the last bus to the village where he and his wife had a cottage. He was truly grateful that we had stopped as he was already wet through and he still had some way to go.

During the journey he explained why he had been delayed on duty. His detachment was seconded to an experimental department which dealt with special aerial dropped missiles. It seemed that one such experimental item had been accidentally dropped by the RAF the previous night. It should have been dropped on a reserved piece of ground some distance from Ardrossan but visibility was bad and the aircrew inexperienced.

He couldn't give much technical information other than to describe, quite accurately, the object he had seen on an RAF trailer earlier the day before on its way to the airfield. Delivering the airman to his cottage we set out to find the experimental establishment where I was soon in consultation with the operations officer who heard my story with much relief.   Apparently weeks of calculations and hard work would have been wasted had my 'mine' not been found.   Giving a 'hitch' in this case turned out to be of great value to all concerned.

Deadly Butterflies

It was many years ago when I was invited to talk to the Road Transport Engineers branch at Lowestoft. The subject of the talk, "All Mine". The evening was very good with a large appreciative audience. Shortly before this engagement I had been awarded the Institute of Road Transport Engineers Speaker of the Year Award, the ceremony being held at the Royal Society of Arts in London.

In my presentation to the engineers I had spoken about German anti personnel bombs and devices. On the overhead projector screen I had my sketch of a Butterfly Bomb and had explained we were not allowed to attempt to render them safe (too many officers had been killed). I explained that we had to remove them by remote control (pulleys and string) then put them in a sand-bagged pit, before blowing them up so they did the least damage. I told them more details would be given about these devices in a book I was attempting to write.

At the end of my presentation came question time which went very well, to everyone's satisfaction. The last question came from an elderly gentleman who said, "These butterfly bombs, do you want one?" to which I replied, jokingly, "Why, do you know where there is one?", "Yes" he said, "there's one hanging up on the ceiling of my bike repair shop. Its been there, untouched since during the war. A local lad brought it in after a German raid when several bombs and incendiaries were dropped. No-one has touched it because we didn't know what it was." "Mind you", he went on, "it's a bit mucky now with dust and spiders webs. It's still yellow though." I strongly advised him to contact the police immediately who would get the Army Bomb Disposal Squad to deal with it. It would certainly be in a very unstable condition after all these years.

After having a drink or two with members and their ladies I dealt with many other questions. Towards the end of the session a very pretty blonde young lady came to me and said, "Lieutenant, you really must write that book". Five minutes later she was back saying, "Please hurry up and write that book". Later I was talking with one of the officials when the pretty blonde returned yet again, putting her arm round my waist she said, "Noel dear, please write that book". I looked into those beautiful eyes and answered, "Yes I expect it will be written posthumously", to which she replied, "Good, the sooner the better" !!!!

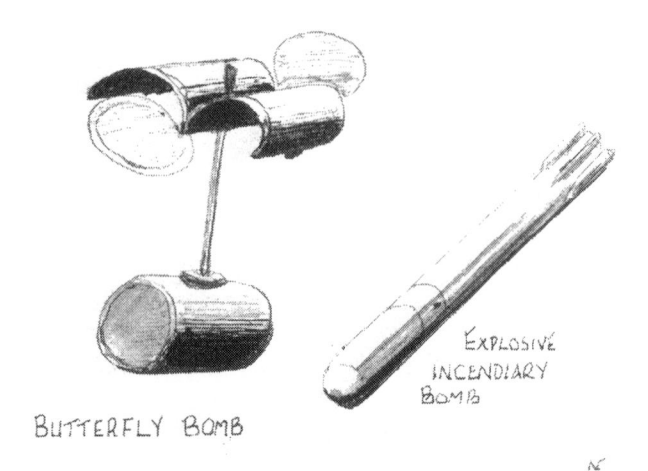

BUTTERFLY BOMB

EXPLOSIVE INCENDIARY BOMB

Oranges Galore
or
I wasn't lucky enough to get whisky!

Two merchant ships left a 'neutral' Spanish port with full cargoes. One day after leaving port the first ship had several internal explosions which eventually caused it to sink. The second ship was two days out into the Atlantic on her way to the UK when suddenly an explosion in the forward hold blew the hatch covers off, one of which slammed into the bridge killing the entire bridge crew.

Surviving crew brought the damaged ship into the Irish Sea and on toward the Clyde. Whilst the ship was still in deep water I was ordered aboard to search the cargo for more explosive devices. Apart from smashed timber and twisted metal work I was instantly aware, as I climbed up the rope ladder from the launch, of a sickly, sweet smell and as my head came above deck level I could see the cause. Everywhere were the spattered remains of hundreds of oranges, up the bridge face, what was left of it, over the deck and rails, covering the derricks, capstans and lines.

Broken hatch cover pieces were in piles where the seamen had stacked them. Down in the hold were cases upon cases of oranges with a crater in the centre, evidence of the seat of the explosion which had done so much damage. The smell of the oranges was almost overwhelming. Wearing my rubber boots and overalls and carrying a small bag of tools I descended into the hold onto the slippery crates.

Starting near the ladder I cut the wire of the nearest crate and with great care removed the oranges searching all the while for anything that was not an orange! All the checked oranges were loaded onto a net sling which, when full was hoisted up to the deck then transferred to lighters which were lying alongside. It took hours to make even a small hole in the cargo. There were a few false alarms, many cups of tea and several duty free cigarettes but progress was being made, albeit slowly.

On the morning of day two some commotion was caused by the stevedores who were supposed to be unloading this ship. They thought that more explosive devices may be in the cargo and stopped work immediately, demanding more danger pay. Negotiations took place but I worked on, emptying crate after crate of very smelly, squashy oranges. When more danger pay was awarded to them the work of unloading recommenced. Honour was satisfied all round. By this time I was well down into the oranges, at times up to the waist in sticky orange juice, my skin was impregnated with a deep orange colour and I looked as though I had a terrible illness.

On the fourth day the hold was almost cleared with just the last corner to do, ten or so layers of crates had been removed. Automatically I opened a crate removing some oranges with my left hand whilst searching carefully with my right when suddenly my fingers touched something that wasn't orange and there neatly packed were several sticks of gelignite with, in the middle of the bundle a black and brown bakelite unit which was evidently the delay mechanism. I quickly blew the whistle, which was on a lanyard round my neck, for the ship (except for key personnel) to be evacuated, and the tugs and lighters moved away to another merchant ship nearby.

It was clear that the device was quite new as, although I had scrutinised every leaflet of explosive devices, none mentioned anything like this. It could not have been very sensitive as I had been kneeling on it for hours clearing the crates around it. Making a drawing of the entire mechanism I passed my notes to the crew member above who then retired to a safer place.

With a sharp knife I cut the tape which embraced each gelignite stick and carefully took one in my very sticky fingers and eased it away from its neighbours, it came away easily and I popped it into a fire bucket which I had with me for this very purpose. I repeated the operation until all the sticks were safely in the bucket and washing my hands in another bucket nearby and drying them on a handkerchief, I eased out the bakelite unit. The words FEDER 504 showed clearly round the widest part. Taking it up to the deck and with great care I started to dismantle the unit. There were a few nasty moments when it sounded as though the clock had started to tick but I managed to isolate the detonating unit from the firing mechanism.

Its teeth were drawn. Having put the gelignite, the bakelite device and the detonator into padded carriage boxes and placing them in the care of a guard I returned to search for any other devices. What seemed like weeks later the holds were emptied and no other devices were found. When I finally left the ship one of the officers presented me with a bottle of Bourbon.

Some weeks later the Boffins who received the FEDER 504 wrote to me saying that the device was timed to explode two days before I got to it. Unknown to me I had been walking over it on and off for at least four days but fortunately the mechanism had been sabotaged during assembly for a tiny disc of film had been inserted which prevented the clock from running its full selected time. I said a silent thank you to the nimble hands which were evidently working unwillingly for an enemy master. They undoubtedly saved me from a decidedly sticky end!

One legacy from this episode is that to this day I do not eat oranges, nor do I care much for their smell and rarely do I drink a glass of orange juice.

Many years after this 'orange job' I heard of another ship from neutral Spain which had also been sabotaged resulting in explosions at sea, finally being searched by another Bomb Disposal Officer in the Clyde.

Initiation into Diving

Upon leaving HMS Volcano as a fully fledged Bomb Disposal Officer my next 'stop' was HMS Vernon at Portsmouth to learn about mines. This took a week followed by a two week course at HMS Excellent, the Naval Gunnery and Diving School, also at Portsmouth. This establishment had the custom that everyone, officers, men and Wrens, were obliged to double, (to the uninitiated - run everywhere!) The discipline was incredible. Gunnery officers were all over the place. All "guts and gaiters" was the expression used. They were a law unto themselves and all quite mad!

One of the activities that did not fill me with unbounded delight was diving. Water and I were not easy companions but there was no-one to whom I could complain so I just had to get on with it. We were taken some three hundred yards off shore in an old tug which had been re-born as a Diver Training Unit. It had no covered accommodation and we stood huddled by the wheelhouse trying to keep warm, the temperature was freezing and the sea, which was choppy, was a miserable grey. The harbour was full of warships and small launches dashed from ship to ship ignoring the red flag on our vessel which signalled to one and all "Keep clear - Diving taking place - reduce speed".

At last I was fitted into a Naval pattern diving suit, sitting on a box whilst my attendant made me comfortable. He tucked in my neck ring which would protect my bony shoulders when the brass corselet and lead weights were hung. These weights were 28lbs the pair and slung on horns on the front and back of the corselet, secured by a light line. The boots were already on and it was my responsibility to secure them with a line in such a way that, should I get into trouble on the sea bed I could quickly release them. The theory being that if I couldn't undo the knots in an emergency and was killed, it would be my own fault and nobody else would be to blame. It certainly taught me the proper way to tie quick release knots and to this day I tie my laces in this way!

The next task was to stand up. With a little help from the diving attendant I made it to the side where the ladder was positioned and, with much effort, managed to swing my leg over the side onto the rung of the ladder only to be faced with the problem of getting the other leg over the side to join its fellow. By this time I was exhausted but knowing how disastrous it would be if I fell into the water at this stage I hung on like grim death.

During all these manoeuvres I was without a helmet, but as soon as I had made it onto the ladder the attendant fitted the contraption over my head with all its cables and hoses attached. With a twist it was locked onto the threads of the corselet. At this stage the face-piece was still to be fitted, the air-pump started rhythmically puffing air from the vent over my right ear. Then the attendant fitted the face-piece which was a threaded brass ring surrounding a disc of thick glass and this was screwed home until it was water tight. The noise in the helmet was deafening but there was no time to panic, gentle pressure on the top of the helmet directed me down each rung of the ladder. Suddenly there were no more rungs but the initial training had been thorough. I transferred my hands from the rungs to the shot rope (this is a thick rope attached to a weight on the sea bed and secured to the ship). The diver uses this as a guide so that when he returns to the surface - eventually and hopefully - he is in the right place.

On this first dive I had to learn how to control the air intake. The danger of allowing too much air into the suit resulted in sudden inflation which blew the suit up like a balloon rendering the diver helpless. If already on the bottom he would be propelled to the surface at great speed where he would lie like a beached whale and have to be rescued by the attending crew!

With the right amount of air in your suit you move as easily as a dancer and my task on this occasion was to go to the bottom, which turned out to be thick oily mud, stay there for twenty minutes and ascend when summoned. So ended the first lesson.

By the end of the course I was still not over thrilled with diving but at least confident in what I was doing, although I did have reservations about the ability to render safe bombs and mines under water as when hands get so cold all feeling goes. It is essential to be able to know what you are doing by touch, since the harbour waters of this country were murky to say the least. One day, no doubt, I would find out if it was possible.

On the day I had to carry out set tasks underwater the weather on the surface was less than pleasant, very cold with snow showers. Underwater it was surprisingly warm. My task was to chop through a chain link using a hammer and cold chisel, not easy but it made me very warm and the visor steamed up. The way to overcome this was to open a small tap on your helmet taking sea water into your mouth through a spout. This was quite difficult as your hands could be frozen with the cold water which resulted in getting rather more water than required. Having managed to get enough water you spray it over the glass. That is the theory but you get most of it in your eyes if you haven't been cute enough to close them and at least you get a wet face which extends down your neck in seconds. But you do have some vision again.

One last task was to undo a bundle of line attached to the base of the shot rope and holding it firmly to walk the full extent of this line. It is not possible for a diver to walk upright in a seaway as the current tends to push him over so a crablike crawl is adopted which allows quite rapid movement. Almost at the end of the line I stood up to adjust the airflow as I was panting rather heavily. There was a strange quiet 'alone' feeling down there at forty feet. Suddenly a movement caught my eye. Coming slowly toward me was the watery ghost of a man dressed in brown workman's overalls. I remembered that a few weeks before German aircraft had attacked the docks and several launches carrying dockyard workers were sunk with heavy losses.

As the figure came closer I was frozen with terror and incapable of moving but slowly reason returned. With my right hand I found the line which held the hammer which was attached to my waist. The ghostly figure seemed as though its arms were going to encircle me, so shutting my eyes and giving a great shout I struck out involuntarily. I encountered something and although frightened had to open my eyes, only to find my ghost was nothing more than a very large piece of corrugated cardboard which by sheer chance was shaped like a human being and the printing on the paper became facial features, I'm sure the encounter aged me a good many years! Needless to say I did not reveal my 'encounter' to the crew above. I'd had more than my fair share of leg-pulling.

More Diving

At Campbeltown there was a large naval base and I was given the task to lecture to the folks there on the perils of anti-personnel bombs, incendiaries and other nasty killing and maiming devices that the Germans were sending us. The lectures took several days to complete but at the end it was discovered that there was no transport to return me to Greenock for another two days so I was left to amuse myself as best I could. Finding myself almost out of toothpaste I wandered into the shopping area and to my surprise bumped into an old shipmate from submarine days. He was serving on an old submarine which was used in conjunction with U-Boat detection and attack training by the newly formed Hunter Groups operating in the Atlantic.

The task allocated to my friend's submarine was to go out into the Irish Sea and act as a U-Boat for the Group to locate on their new listening equipment and generally they returned the following day. He suggested that I join them when they left that afternoon as I had two days to 'kill' and he thought it would be interesting for me to see what they were doing. Departure time was 1600 hours (4 pm.)

Returning to my billet I called into the duty officer's room and explained the circumstances. Commander Buckley was there and agreed that as I had completed my mission I was free until getting transport back to Greenock. Going to the room which had been allocated to me for my stay I unpacked my thick submariner's jersey from my case and put it on, packed my toilet gear and went down the stairs. The Commander's door was open and he called me in. "Cashford, you do realise that once you are on that submarine we cannot get you back until it returns off exercise and if we get a visit from Jerry bombers or you are wanted back at Greenock, there could be one hell of a stink. Think about it, but I leave it to you".

Not a lot of thought was needed as it was clear that we could both be in a lot of trouble so I returned to my room, took off my submarine gear and hurried to the dock side to tell my friend the decision, only to find that the submarine had already left its mooring and was making its way out to sea. I did manage to wave to him.

Upon returning to Greenock I spent a lot of time practicing rendering safe various German bomb fuses which we had obtained and it was about ten days later that I was ordered to report to the Diving School at HMS Excellent at Portsmouth. For the first week I occupied what had been the cabin of one of the ladies-in-waiting on board the Royal Yacht Victoria and Albert which was used as a floating sleeping quarters for visiting officers.

Three days after arriving I did my first dive in Portsmouth harbour. Any modern films showing beautiful clear water and clean sea bed - please forget! The water where I dived was so dirty the visibility was less than five feet (that's with the sun shining) and the sea bed was three to four feet deep in dirty soft mud which becomes like thick soup when disturbed by even careful divers. My Petty Officer instructor was excellent and quite a celebrity in the diving world having achieved the deepest dive in a normal Admiralty pattern suit.

Diving was taking place from an old tug which had been equipped for the purpose. The morning was clear and early frost made everything extremely cold, so much so that the assistant who was helping me to don my suit and fix the brass corset on my shoulders ready for the helmet, had to break the ice on the water in the bucket which contained the securing nuts!

The Petty Officer and I sat on a bench whilst he briefed me on what I was to do when I entered the water. There was another diver already down so I had to wait about an hour until he was back on board the diving boat. Only one diver was allowed down at this stage of training. I got very cold and my hands were freezing causing me to remark about this to the instructor. Looking around him carefully to make sure he could not be heard because of the warning that "Careless talk costs lives" he quietly said (for my ears only) "Its not so cold here as where I have been". Asking where this was he told me he had been on a rotten job on the west coast of Scotland where one of our old submarines had sunk after exercising with Hunter Groups and all hands had been lost.

Feeling very troubled I reached into my jacket pocket which contained my diary and, sure enough, it was the day after Commander Buckley advised me not to go out on the submarine with my ex shipmate. She failed to return and all the ship's company had perished. You can imagine how I felt because, if it had not been for Commander Buckley I would have been on that submarine! Commander Buckley's is one name I shall never forget.

Even More Diving

Although there existed three sizes of Admiralty pattern divers suits; large, medium and small, they always issued me with a large one which was excessively large for my small frame. After shooting to the surface from a depth of fifty or sixty feet and out of control of the air release valve because my helmet had risen above my reach on leaving the sea bed, I got quite annoyed!

At that time I was senior in rank, not age, to the Chief Petty Officer in charge of diving and after three consecutive 'blow ups' which shot me to the surface like a rocket leaving me stretched out floating and helpless, I pulled rank. To the reader my advice is no matter what your position is, never pull rank on a junior rank.

This is what happened. Whilst I was stretched out on the surface they unceremoniously towed me to the diving boat and a seaman with a broom came down the divers ladder and, reaching down to a spit cock in the chin area of the diving helmet, opened it, letting the air gush out, while at the same time pushing my legs down with the broom head so that I did not descend head first to the sea bed. The whole incident was highly embarrassing for me and after I had regained the deck of the diving boat and the face piece had been removed I was able to vent my anger. Calling the C.P.O. over I proceeded to give him a right good telling off for issuing me with too large a diving suit. He listened po-faced and then said "Alright Sir, I'll fix it".

Returning to the Diving Station after a light lunch another large suit was awaiting me. The seaman assistant told me that the Chief had arranged something - I should have been wary then. When dressed and with the helmet on the Chief arrived with a 3 inch wide leather strap which he passed between my legs securing the ends to the horns on the back and front of the corset. Peering into my helmet with beer laden breath he said "I fixed it, Sir".

Going to the side to commence the dive I climbed onto the ladder and stood there whilst the attendant fitted the face piece and screwed it into place. Then stopping on the bottom rung waited for the tap on the helmet to tell me there were no obvious leaks in my gear. Finding the shot rope I descended to an anchor on the sea bed about 50 feet below and carried out further experience training as directed from above. The messages were conveyed by various tugs on the air line cable.

After half an hour or more I got the message to surface urgently so I immediately stopped air from leaving the suit by reaching up and closing the valve situated on the right side of the helmet. Air came rushing in from above and quickly filled the suit. In seconds the excessive tucks of the suit around my waist began to fill and the helmet lifted off my shoulders, the sleeves filled with air making my arms immovable and level with my shoulders.

The leather band so carefully placed by the Chief Petty Officer now became a steel vice between my legs and the pain was excruciating, I remember screaming and was aware that I was rushing uncontrolled to the surface where I shot out like a rocket and fell back with a splash, to lie there on the surface. I must have blacked out as I came to slumped on the deck of the diving boat and the diving suit was being hurriedly pulled off.

For many weeks I was black and blue in a very sensitive area but I eventually recovered. It amazed me years later when first Michael and 4 years after him, Peter arrived!!!

A week later I dived again and 4 weeks after that passed the test, but never again was I issued with a large suit nor did I ever 'pull rank' again. Incidentally the proficiency test was to dive deep, search and find a concrete block to which was secured a chain (about the size of a large dog chain). The sixth link had to be removed using a chisel and hammer, which even in air is a strenuous task. Just try it under water, your hammer blow has to push through the water to impact the head of the chisel. After a very short time I had generated so much perspiration the inside of the suit was running with water for not only were the tasks to be performed but the testers above were gauging my reactions to circumstances (i.e. how quickly I closed off the air release valve when they stopped the pump pushing vital air into the suit - plus several other nasty events.) Only when the chain had been parted was the diver allowed to the surface.

One question frequently asked is "What happens to a diver on the sea bed when he wants to urinate?" What do you think? This much I will say, naval divers have to wash and dry the suit and gear they have worn at the end of each diving session!!

Refreshers

Some months later, whilst working with UXB's, etc. I was again at HMS Vernon, Portsmouth for a refresher course on booby traps which had been introduced into mines and bombs by the enemy. Having finished the course I was granted a few days leave.

The journey home turned out to be an epic experience. The train from Portsmouth to Brighton departed on time at 3 p.m. where I should be able to get the 5 p.m. train to Tunbridge Wells. Alas because of sneak low level German raids on the Sussex coast the train was stationary for hours. We eventually arrived at Brighton at 7.30 p.m. My next connection wasn't until after midnight. This train did depart on time although it had very few passengers, but I spent a pleasant journey with a pretty Wren who was going on leave to Tonbridge. As I recall she was, as she described it, a cub reporter on a Tonbridge newspaper. I had intended to make a date but can't remember if I did!

We arrived at Tunbridge Wells station and for me there was nothing for it but to trudge three miles home, with my heavy suitcase. The time then being nearly two a.m. Fortunately it was a fine night.

Now here's the peculiar bit. About three quarters of an hour earlier, Bruce woke my mother from her deep slumbers, rushed downstairs to the back door (which I always used) and sat there whimpering. Several times he repeated this. Eventually Mother put on her dressing gown and slippers and followed him to the back door. Bruce would not budge, so, Mother put the kettle on for the inevitable cup of tea adding another cup to the tray for, as she said, Bruce told her to expect a visitor.

I arrived 20 minutes or so later, quietly opening and closing the gate so as not to disturb the neighbours. When I opened the unlocked door Bruce went crazy with ecstasy and I was almost licked to death. He was an amazing dog with his ability to sense oncoming raids and, also, his sixth sense when a member of the family was on their way home.

Sadly, about two years later, beautiful Bruce fell victim to distemper. I had a few hours spare whilst on a course in London so I rushed home. Poor Bruce was seriously ill and as I was getting ready to leave again I stroked his head as he lay on his sick bed. He raised his head, gave one of his 'I love you' whimpers and died. Mother and I cried for ages, but I had to pull myself together as I had to get the train back to London to duty at HQ where I was supposed to learn deciphering. I failed badly for I couldn't see the paper for tears.

The Wren Officer must have thought I was 'bomb happy' or simple. I couldn't tell her I was mourning a beautiful dog named Bruce. There were too many people around mourning the loss of loved ones who were bomb victims. My loss was trivial compared to theirs.

Smoke Screen in Plymouth Docks

Guest nights in the wardroom in Devonport were occasions one could enjoy. The richness of the table decorations were an eye opener. Solid silver working models of gun carriages were paraded round the tables. They were worth a King's Ransom. Diligent stewards ensured that their charges were properly turned out and the build up was exciting.

On one of the 'nights', due to lack of communication, I was not aware that I was on duty and had thrown myself into the spirit of the evening with gusto. Some of the guests were jovial chaps recently returned from a long spell in the Mediterranean. Three of the bods were placed, two on one side of me and one on the other, and we had really enjoyed the evening with rather a lot of 'liquid refreshment'.

The evening was almost over and most of the guests had departed or gone to bed when the sirens started their wailing. It was an air raid, Red Alert. One of my colleagues came to me and asked if he should have my motorcycle brought round to which I asked "Why?" "Because", he said, "you are duty Bomb & Mine Disposal Officer tonight!"

By the time it had all been sorted out, the smoke screen barrage was in full swing. This was a screen of dense smoke which was put over the docks so that individual areas, buildings, ships, etc. could not be picked out from the air. Anti-aircraft guns from east of Plymouth had also opened up followed by some heavy guns from large ships in the Dockyard. Quickly I changed into working gear and putting my gas mask case over my shoulder, went out to where my colleague was standing with the motor bike, which was quietly ticking over.

The sky was full of bursting anti-aircraft shells and by the time I had ridden to the dockyard and passed the police point, the smoke, which was a horrible brown, was so thick visibility was down to about three or four feet. Having difficulty breathing, I stopped for a moment frightened that we were having a gas attack. It was imperative that I reached the Passive Defence HQ which organised incidents reported and ordered counter action, such as dealing with any bombs which failed to explode or parachute mines that landed. My job was to be ready at a moments notice to deal with these incidents.

Knowing that the rails (which were sunken into the road) for the dockyard trains ran all the way to HQ, I decided to get into one and follow it round as it would eventually lead me to my destination. Carefully I revved my trusty stead and drove along at a steady 15 mph. All was going well, apart from the continuous barrage from the anti-aircraft guns which did not bother me much.

HQ should soon be appearing, a curve to the right came up which I remembered. I knew the road fairly well, or so I thought. The road did a gradual turn to the right around a dock, a turn to left then straight on. As there were several junctions to be negotiated I had put my feet to the road to steady the bike.

Suddenly another large bang, which was too near to be comfortable, made me realize I should have to don my tin hat. Then it happened. The front wheel seemed to drop into space and the frame of the bike cracked into something. The handle bars turned too easily but my feet were either side on the road holding the bike upright. By this time I was completely sober and very scared as I discovered the bike and I were poised at the end of a dock, almost at the point of no return. Nearby was the stern of an armed merchant cruiser firing her guns like mad. The murky water was waiting for me some twenty feet below so with super human effort I dragged the machine back to safety. Shaking like a leaf I continued to Passive Defence on foot after abandoning the bike on the dock. What had happened, as I found out by retracing my steps in daylight, was I had followed a rail that had terminated on the dock edge but had no buffers!!!

Eventually I arrived at HQ, two hours late for duty. I was informed that the air raid was a false alarm and no enemy had been closer than sixty miles. Needless to say, I was so shaken that I parted company with my excellent dinner!

"D" Day 1944

In preparation for 'D' Day I was sent from Plymouth to Fowey, Cornwall. It was a boring period but I did get along the coast occasionally to attend to several unidentified objects which washed ashore. These turned out to be mostly harmless smoke floats or markers dropped by aircraft.

On one occasion a small harbour village was evacuated because what appeared to be a mine had washed up onto the beach nearby. My BSA motorcycle got me to the scene in under the hour. The object was a four foot diameter sphere. It was not a mine or explosive of any sort, just a buoy which presumably had come from the Spanish coast and washed ashore in Cornwall. It was later pulled out of harms way by a local scrap metal dealer!

About a month later a bomb was reported, by the police, near the promenade at Mevagissey. Again my trusty motorbike got me there at record speed. It was my first visit to Mevagissey. As I sought the police or coast guard I walked along the front. I was amazed. The shop fronts had a wooden construction covering many of them and painted in an earlier architecture.

Several people were grouped around one place. As I walked along a small 'round' man in a dark suit and wearing a bowler hat came trotting toward me, exclaiming as he approached, "You'll do fine". I challenged, "What would I do fine?" He explained that he was making a film "Johnny Frenchman" and in one scene a naval officer was to approach another launch containing French smugglers. I would be standing in the bow of the British launch and one of the French, when near enough, would knock me into the sea. This was enough for me and I told him in best Naval language to 'B.O'. He threatened that as he knew my boss, the Commander at Fowey, he would get me ordered to do this bit of film. I left him standing there and went on to do my job, the object turned out to be a harmless smoke float and no danger. I hastened back to Fowey and reported events to the Commander. He just chuckled. That was the end of the extraordinary episode, and I haven't seen the film. I often wonder if I turned down a brilliant future in films I rather doubt it.

Soon 'D' Day occurred and I returned to Plymouth to clear up bomb sites, etc and to start clearing various live ammunition battle sites which had been used as practice ground in preparation for that enormous and successful undertaking in Europe.

Dredger Drama

When there was a lull in 'objects to be rendered safe' the bomb disposal crews were given the task of clearing partly exploded bomb fragments which littered areas of Plymouth after bombing raids. This involved digging around craters collecting pieces of bombs, some of which still retained traces of yellowish explosive. The soil was clay and had the consistency of glue which stuck to the spades when we tried to throw the stuff out of the crater. Hard going but we were doing a good and important job.

Meanwhile, in the dockyard, a large dredger was keeping the channels open as usual. This was essential work as the ships must be able to get into the dockyard at anytime. One of the crew suddenly saw what looked like a large bomb in one of the buckets. He raised the alarm and the dredger was immediately stopped and quickly moved alongside the wall where all crew 'abandoned ship' and the police cleared and sealed the area. A motorcycle messenger found my party and within 10 minutes we were in Devonport dockyard alongside the dredger where it took but seconds to determine that the bomb was in fact a magnetic mine with its parachute still attached.

Although the whole bucket and its contents were covered in a layer of filthy grey mud, the fuses were just visible and it was apparent that on its descent to the sea bed it had struck something hard which had caused the tops of the fuses to be very badly damaged. First rigging a hosepipe my crew then retreated to the regulation safe distance and I proceeded to hose the bucket and contents clean.

The mine looked gigantic and it was clear that the damage to the fuses would make any normal method of rendering safe impossible. Before I could proceed any further my boss had to be contacted as, strictly speaking, this was a case for the Naval Land Incident Section. In general they dealt with parachute mines. Twenty minutes later I was instructed to evacuate my crew and self and wait at a safe distance until someone from Havant arrived. Three hours later, and with the kind assistance of the Fleet Air Arm, Sub Lt W. arrived. Casting his expert eye over the mine he came to the same conclusion that the fuses were too badly damaged to attempt removal of the fuse mechanism. The mine had already been snatched from thirty feet of water and had taken a fair beating by the time it surfaced.

It was his decision, but in consultation we discussed the options and the one chosen was to carefully lift the mine from the dredger bucket into our Bomb Disposal truck and rapidly drive out to the moors where we would blow it up. We watched as our 'charge' was lifted, without too many problems, where it was placed amongst our spades and Bomb Disposal gear into the rear of the truck and there it was securely wedged.

With army and police escorts ahead clearing the way we raced out of the dockyard through the evacuated streets of Devonport toward the moors. The torrential rain had stopped and the sun came out drying the wet roads quickly. I was riding rearguard on my motorcycle and was about twenty feet behind the truck. The convoy was passing through a very built up area when I noticed smoke issuing from the rear of the truck!

At first I assumed it was exhaust but soon changed my mind when flames flickered. There was more smoke making it difficult to see where the fire was coming from. Closing up to the truck I could smell the distinct odour of burning explosives. Accelerating alongside the truck I managed to alert the driver, who had not noticed the smoke trail he was leaving.

Motioning him to follow me I led him about a quarter of a mile further on where I knew of an open area with few houses that were standing. Arriving in the middle of the area we stopped. Running to the back of the truck I lowered the tail board and there could see the source of our fire. One of the sacks was smouldering which I threw as far away as possible, then as I lifted one of the spades out the handle promptly burst into flames. The wet sack quickly put it out but it burst into flames again.

Closer examination revealed the cause. Remember we had been called away from the bomb site to attend the dredger incident and had thrown our gear into the back of the truck in our haste to get to the scene as quickly as possible. Well, this meant that much of the material was soaking wet because of the torrential rain when we loaded. But now the sun was out. It was obvious that the bombs we had been dealing with were phosphorus incendiaries and the wet clay had acted as an insulator and when that dried and air got to the explosive it burst into flames. The speed of the truck had assisted the drying of the clay causing our predicament. We made great haste to clean the tools and the floor of the truck and as an extra precaution one of the crew rode in the back with fire buckets we had 'borrowed' from somewhere ready to douse any flames that may appear. In this way we continued our eventful journey to the moors. Arriving at the quarry we were going to use for the demolition, we made haste to prepare the mine first making sure there were no aircraft in the area. Having done this we disposed of our troublesome magnetic mine and after clearing up returned to base in Plymouth.

The following morning I was summoned to appear before the 'powers that be' to receive what is known in the Navy as a rocket. When I turned the truck off the planned route onto the waste ground the army and police escorts who were leading did not notice us disappear. After a while they realised we were not with them and stopped to wait for us and by sheer coincidence witnessed a large bang about a mile from them. There was much smoke and debris and they concluded that it was our truck that had gone sky high. After a while they sadly rode back to base and reported the incident.

In actual fact what they had seen was the Royal Engineers demolishing dangerous buildings which had been bombed sometime earlier. In retrospect I realised someone should have been notified but we were rather 'tied up' with our smoking mine!!!

Twice I worked on dredgers, the other occasion was in Dover harbour but that, as they say, is another story.

Studland Battle Range

One of the saddest events during my time as a Bomb & Mine Disposal Officer occurred during the clearance of the Battle Range at Studland. The purpose of our trips to that beautiful place was to clear all unexploded missiles fired into the area and dropped from the air during training exercises by Allied troops for a landing from the sea. Most of us were lodged in a Temperance Hotel in West Bournemouth. It was definitely 'dry' and furthermore we were not supposed to be out after 10.30 p.m. otherwise we were locked out. Needless to say we soon had a spare key, much to the annoyance of the staid proprietors. They were nice folk in their way, so we respected them as much as was humanly possible.

On one visit to Studland we had with us a French Canadian Paul S. We knew he was completely mad when we first saw him. He sported a naval beard and set which was quite definitely not British Naval style! It was almost bright red, the upper set on his lip had the ends so regularly twisted they turned up some four inches and the lower half was split centrally and came to two points. The whole looked much as you would expect Satan to look. The horns could well have been hidden by a scruffy hat with a gold badge which was a dirty green shade.

One Sunday evening, three of us, including Paul S walked to the main promenade garden area heading for the pub which (supposedly) had some beer. All the garden seats were occupied as it was one of those rare occasions, a warm sunny evening. As we came to a path junction a seat faced us upon which sat an elderly lady. As she saw us approaching she registered astonishment at Paul's appearance. She nudged her sleepy male companion and he also seemed mesmerised by the apparition before him. Paul saw their reaction and, leaving us, he skipped ahead in a dainty dance right over to the elderly couple, whereupon he bent towards the lady and thrust his chin almost into her face and with palms uppermost supporting his beard, said in his broken English, "Isn't it lurvly". With that the lady stood up, snorted and dragged her male companion away, convinced I imagine that a madman had got loose.

After Paul had a few pints he became really friendly, told us he had been a gun runner in South America, where things got hot so he joined the Canadian Navy to get away for a time. He was disgusted to be sent to this dangerous country and he announced that he did not intend to work on explosives as that was far too dangerous. Paul was very sociable most of the time, albeit eccentric. He painted a word picture of his beautiful wife Simone back home in Quebec. He couldn't contain his emotions and the tears ran down his chin into his beer stained whiskers. He then took out his wallet and proceeded to show all and sundry photographs of Simone. Each snapshot was in colour and was of a plump, quite naked female in different poses - some quite erotic. Paul was unashamed at the reaction of some of the RAF aircrew who had joined us.

The next day Paul had to come with us to the sand dunes of Studland. He refused to work and we were glad not to have him around as he was certainly "round the bend". We spent hours prodding the sand and uncovering miscellaneous unexploded devices. Some rocket heads had to have the fuses rendered safe and then recovered in order to return them to the factory who made them to ascertain why they had failed. These were tricky jobs to say the least but we did not mind, especially when the weather was good and at lunchtime, when we drove from the range into Studland. There, hidden in a pinewood, was a once peacetime restaurant, the proprietor of which prepared excellent meals for us at extremely low prices. She and her helpers were much appreciated by us all at that time as you can imagine.

At the end of one busy week when work stopped and all tools were collected, we started walking towards the ferry at Sandbanks. One of our colleagues was off on leave that evening and his spirits were very high. He was to meet his 18 year old daughter whom he had not seen for many years. She was being repatriated by the Red Cross from Germany where she had been at school at the outbreak of war. At that time T C was employed by a German Shipping Line based at Hamburg. Early in 1938 he had left Germany for the Far East where he was when war was declared. He managed to jump ship and eventually came to England.

Whilst the party was walking toward the distant ferry T C lagged behind. It seems he kicked a cardboard coated lump, which he recognised as a lump of TNT from a practice bomb which had broken up on impact. He had some cotton waste and a tin of paraffin with him. The party hadn't missed him. One of the party turned round and saw him pouring paraffin from his tin onto this lump which was about the size of a cushion. The rest of us walked on. Some minutes later there was a terrific explosion and turning round we were all horrified at what we witnessed. There, some 500 yards away, through the sand storm created by the explosion could be seen this dark sitting shape. They ran back as the sand gradually settled. In front of them was a crater in the sand about twenty feet across, some five feet deep. On the edge sat a pathetic shape of what was once a handsome six foot Royal Naval Reserve Sub Lieutenant. His badly mauled body was taken to hospital where survival was not expected but, months and months of devoted nursing by hospital staff eventually made it possible for him to come out of intensive care. I remember his excitement at the thought of being able to see his grown up daughter. This was his main desire from the moment he learned that the Red Cross were helping to effect repatriation.

Sadly, T C lost his sight at Studland.

Stars & Stripes

The U.S. Navy had a base in Fowey. They were the famous Sea Bees. It was their task to prepare the invasion beaches for landing well before the main event. A highly dangerous task with high mortality rate. I was introduced to the explosives officer, Lt. Ralph Palumbo, a super guy with an obvious Italian background. I found the whole US crew excellent chaps and got to know them well. We did mock exercises together. They gave me some of their demolition explosives and tools when they saw my inferior issue.

Ralph's constant companion was a small dog. To describe it is not easy, he looked more like a elongated grey mop than a dog. You guessed where his head was by the direction he was going and his name was Bomber. He had been taught many tricks and would recover items better than a retriever. One of his tricks still leaves me pondering. Ralph, Bomber and I with a petty officer, drove to a remote sandy beach, Bomber being commanded to stay in the vehicle behind a sand dune. With six 1¼ pound tins of TNT explosive we walked onto the sands toward the on coming tide. Petty Officer Nelson (yes, that was his name) dug a hole with his hands and buried a TNT tin, repeating this five times more along the sand. All were covered and it was not possible to detect them.

Ten minutes later Bomber was released from the vehicle and instructed to find. Ralph went within approximately six feet from the general area where the TNT tins had been placed. After quarter of an hour Bomber scratched up his first tin, was rewarded with a cookie and proceeded to find the rest. Ralph's next training session was to get Bomber to sit near to the target and bark, for if he had scratched or attempted movement it may have been booby trapped and explode. He was a very clever wee dog.

During my quiet times I fished thousands of mackerel in the harbour, all of which went to the hospital. I had other duties which were too boring to mention. The U.S Navy were always generous. They held some good 'At Homes', plenty of white bread, unlimited meats, butter, cheese, etc. They were popular events. I escorted a pretty Wren officer to one. When we arrived we were asked to have a drink, of course we agreed. To my surprise on a counter bar stood three stainless steel buckets. The steward got two large tumblers in his hand, scooped them through each bucket in turn and handed us the dripping glasses. It was full of gin, grapefruit juice and chipped ice.

The inevitable dance music was playing and after another of those drinks, even I non dancer that I am, joined my Wren friend. Within an hour I had introduced my Wren to most of the U.S. Navy Officers and then back to smooching. It was whilst this was taking place that a junior officer grabbed the Wren and started to throw her about in his version of jitterbugging. It was plain she was very unhappy about this so I went and said the customary excuse me. He turned on me and told me to beat it. Of course I didn't. His right hand went to his left armpit and at that moment Ralph came up. He told the Ensign to go and get him a drink which the fellow did immediately. Don't tangle with that guy he advised, he's already killed a chap in the States and always has a Derringer automatic in an arm holster. He is the son of a Senator.

My Wren friend and I soon went to our respective billets. Apart from that incident it was an entertaining evening.

Bomber

Dangerous Cricket

Before the Second Front began I was stationed in Fowey in Cornwall and one day I was sent for by the local Naval Officer in charge. The task he had for me was to act as escort to some ladies from the W.V.S. who had been given the use of a Naval launch to go outside the harbour and along the shoreline to the west of the town. The object of the exercise was to collect some special type of seaweed which was used in the culture of the then new wonder drug Penicillin. To say I was not too happy about this duty is an understatement but I was reminded that the operation was vital to our war efforts and I must accompany the ladies and see that they came to 'no harm'. I really could not see how I, unarmed as I was, could counter any armed intervention by anyone, U-Boats, pirates or whatever!

On the appointed afternoon the launch arrived at the town steps and the fifteen or so ladies climbed aboard. It was one of those glorious days with hardly a cloud in the sky and the warm sun shining since early morning with the sea almost flat calm. By the time we had gone through the primitive sea defence boom into the seaway a light swell upset a few of the ladies and several faces turned rather grey, including mine.

Fortunately it did not take long to reached calm water again which was a few yards off the rocky shore where "Operation Seaweed" was to take place. The launch was run into a sandy bay between the large rocks and the ladies, plus their sacks, climbed down the ladder to the beach and quickly set about collecting huge quantities of wet seaweed of a very special kind. For most of the time I found the trip pleasant but did get rather fed-up with the constant chatter of the ladies. After a while they climbed back on board and we moved to other seaweed strewn pastures. By four o'clock, yours truly was more than fed-up but because this was 'duty' I busied myself collecting the precious seaweed and carrying the laden sacks to the launch where they were stowed in the stern. I also reasoned to myself that the sooner the task was completed, the quicker we could get back to town!.

The task took longer than anticipated and it was all of 5 o'clock before it was considered we had collected sufficient. By now we were quite close to town and I reckoned that, as the crow flies, it was only about a mile to walk back to my billet which was at the Riverside Hotel in Fowey. I saw the ladies safely back onto the launch and away into the channel on their journey back to Fowey.

Hopping from rock to rock I eventually reached dry sand where some thirty or so feet away was a meadow. As I strode across the sand some movement caught my eye and it quickly revealed itself as about eight or so men in RAF uniform busy playing a form of cricket. Behind them up a small hill was a caravan, two or three camouflage trucks and, close to the ground, the unmistakable shape of a barrage balloon.

It was obvious that the 'cricketers' were the crew manning the balloon site. It was not clear which of the overgrown paths would take me back to Fowey so I approached the wicket keeper and at this moment the bowler spotted me. Stopping in mid bowl he came over and asked "What are you doing here Sir?".

He was a sergeant so I returned his salute and asked the way to Fowey. This NCO was no fool. Although none of the airmen was armed they sensed something odd, and when you think about it, it was! A naval officer suddenly appears, seemingly out of the sea and asks a question like that. The players surrounded me and the batsman held his bat rather too much like an offensive weapon for my liking. Hastily explaining how and where I came from and what I had been involved in for the past four hours, it seems the sergeant was satisfied that I was speaking the truth so he gave directions for the correct path to reach Fowey.

Thanking him and wishing them all a "good game" I set off in the direction indicated which took me near to the only "wicket" being used. For seconds I could not believe my eyes for the wicket was a conical steel shaped device about a metre high with its base about half a metre in diameter which was resting on a man-made sand heap some third of a metre high by a metre wide. What I was seeing was either a harmless German conical float or a very lethal and very sensitive German explosive conical float! Very few of the latter had been seen other than by captured German naval photographs.

Frequently the non-explosive floats washed ashore but recently some had been seen to blow-up on touching land. These devices were used by the Germans to protect their minefields and when our minesweepers attempted to sweep, the explosive floats would tangle with the sweep wires and literally blow up and make an awful mess of the minesweeper as it passed overhead. It seemed to me I had stumbled on a 'hornets nest' and hastily commanded the airmen to retreat to a safe distance explaining at the same time what their wicket most probably was - needless to say they didn't believe me!!!

In the end I had to pull rank. The single gold braid round my cuff was sufficient to make them obey and reluctantly they retreated up the hill to their base. Gingerly I scraped the sand under the base hoping that this was the common simple float. With shaking fingers more sand was removed, not too much or the thing would topple over. When enough was cleared it was obvious that this was a DEADLY EXPLOSIVE CONICAL FLOAT.

I was still on my knees replacing the sand carefully around the float to keep it steady when there was a very angry bellowing from behind me. As I stood up and turned there was an extremely tall junior RAF officer bearing down on me, his face red with rage; "What the **?!* do you think you are doing, stopping my men from their well earned recreation?" He went on to say that he would report me to the Naval Officer in Charge who, he added, he happened to know. I had to almost physically drag him away from the danger area. In the end efforts to explain myself were accepted and I was able to get a message to base and from then on maximum co-operation. Sentries were posted and the whole area cordoned off lest any off duty airmen or unauthorised persons strayed into the danger area. The Flight Lieutenant then took me to the caravan to meet his wife who quickly made some tea.

The RAF truck was mustered to take me into Fowey to my stores on the town quay where I collected my demolition box and tools then, with all speed, returned to the balloon site.

By this time the evening sun was obscured by heavy storm clouds and the wind was freshening to what seemed, at times, almost gale force which was the last thing needed and, as I approached the lethal 'wicket', I'll swear it rocked. If it was going to fall I hoped it would be before I was too close as the freshening wind could be the death of me! Returning to the balloon site I borrowed three angle iron stakes, on military lists (barbed wire for the use of) some string and a large hammer. Back at the float I hammered the three stakes into the turf around the object about 6 feet distant. They were nice and firm and upright. String was tied from the top of one stake to the top of the float (with great care) and then to each of the other stakes and back to the float in turn so it was held firmly.

It was at this point another hazard manifested itself. The high wind was blowing the sand away from the bottom of the float and it was doubtful how long it would remain safe. Very quickly I prepared a gelignite charge which would blow up the explosive in the float and scraped away the sand near the explosive container so the gelignite charge could rest tightly against it.

Replacing the sand covering the charge I added two or three buckets of sand just to make things more secure. Everything was ready, the sentries were checked and told to take cover and the entire area scanned. Allowing 1 minute of time fuse and with a few inches of it exposed I was ready to light it with a match. I fired the red Very Light which warned those at the balloon site and the sentries that in one minute a detonation would take place.

The cover I had selected was a large tree trunk some 25 yards away and once more the area was thoroughly scanned - no sign of life so I applied the match to the fuse core which spluttered and lit. Picking up my gear I trotted over toward the shore to my cover. Almost there I heard the now familiar voice of the RAF officer who was running down to the 'cricket pitch'. Shouting at him to take cover I ran past the float, now emitting smoke from the burning fuse and reached the chap, grabbed him by the arm and literally dragged him to some fairly large rocks on the beach which, with luck, would afford some cover for both of us from the shrapnel about to fly.

Crouching down, with my knees in a couple of inches of the incoming tide I glanced at my companion who had, like me knelt down, but suddenly he stood almost upright, all 'ten feet' of him. There was an enormous crack and great pieces of twisted steel shot skywards and once more I screamed at him to take cover, which he did and, as I watched, a very large piece of metal slowly spun, about head height, between the rocks behind which we were sheltering and dropped a couple of feet from where the chap was bending and there it sizzled as it cooled in the water, giving off clouds of steam. To say I was angry was the understatement of the century. Not only had his stupid action put him at risk but myself also. An awful lot had taken place in the minute it took the fuse to burn!

It took a few moments for the fellow to realise how stupid he had been, then he went whiter than white and shook so uncontrollably that he could hardly speak. As it was now all clear and perfectly safe I fired a green Very light and led the shaking officer to where his wife was waiting at the door of their caravan with the inevitable cup of tea. Within half an hour the Flight Lieutenant had regained his composure and, whilst I enjoyed a gin and tonic, he walked with his wife down to the erstwhile 'cricket pitch'. When he returned he was scowling "Well all I can say is that thanks to you our pitch is unusable." I didn't say a word.

Twenty minutes later as I was about to climb into the cab of the RAF truck which was to take me back to Fowey town I turned to him and asked why he had come running into the demolition area after the warning shot was fired. His reply knocked me sideways. "I came to ask if you would like another cup of tea." So I guess his heart was in the right place anyway!! Another thought struck me as the truck bumped its way back to Fowey, what a lot I should have missed if I'd gone back in the launch with the ladies. There may have been several dead and badly injured RAF 'cricketers'. It may seem fanciful, but it seems as though I was meant to take the action I did!

Stumped

Battle Ranges
Torcross and Startpoint 1945

There was one aspect of my job I disliked above all others and that was dealing with small bombs or grenade type devices. Too often colleagues had been maimed by just a few ounces of explosives and I dreaded the thought of losing a limb or, worse still, my sight or becoming, as some people had, virtual cabbages due to brain injuries. I hoped that if it was my fate to be blown up that it would be a complete job, with vaporisation, then nobody would have the dreadful task of 'picking up the pieces'. So the next account covers a very traumatic experience.

Early in 1945 I was given the task of clearing the battle ranges at Torcross and Startpoint. This was an enormous undertaking as the American Forces had practiced landings in preparation for the Second Front using live ammunition and, on top of all that, the beaches were heavily defended with scaffolding, mines and other 'nasties'. Another task I had was of removing pill-boxes, but more of that later.

First and foremost I had to clear the scaffolding of mines which, due to the years of constant pounding by water, sand and shingle much deterioration had been caused to the structure, so it was with great care that I began the task of removal. Scaffolding mines had been fixed about every 20 feet or so at differing levels and were in various conditions of safety.

For days the work went smoothly, safety pins were placed and the mine fuses carefully removed after which the defused mines were unbolted by my crew who followed at a safe distance. It was when we came to areas where not only the weather had caused deterioration in the scaffolding but the live ammunition used in the invasion training had also done much damage and some of the structure had collapsed completely, which meant that mines which had not exploded at the time, fell down to be covered by sand every time the tide came in. Where this had happened I had problems!

Mine detectors could not be used owing to the vast amount of loose metal around the place so I gingerly probed the sand with brass rods. If I touched something solid I moved a few inches probing carefully until the outline could be seen. If it was approximately 12 inches diameter the assumption had to be that it was a mine. The next move was to clear the sand and, with luck, it would be easy to render safe. This work took a long time as I had to go so very slowly and one bright morning everything was going just fine. Every mine was intact and easy to reach, it took only a few seconds to insert the safety pins and remove the fuses. Some were a bit difficult but by and large things were going well.

I was dealing with one of the lowest mines which was about four feet above the sand when I suddenly lost my footing on the scaffolding. I tried to put the fuse into the box hanging from the scaffolding but it fell out and descended with me. As I hit the sand I felt a movement beneath my left foot, at the same time the fuse hit the base

C TYPE BEACH MINE ANTI TANK.

of the scaffolding but, thankfully, did not explode but just lay there, very rusty except for a bright metal scar on its side.

My next concern was, on what had I landed? What was it that moved as if it was spring loaded? For what seemed ages I did not move then decided I would have to. Carefully I lifted my left foot and heard a muffled crack as metal scraped on metal. I moved again and nothing happened! Within seconds I had removed the sand and small shells and there, in all its glory, was a scaffolding mine which I very respectfully lifted out. With difficulty I placed a safety pin and removed the fuse where I laid it carefully next to its fallen companion.

Why hadn't the mine exploded when yours truly dropped onto it? I stripped it out (I simply had to know) and found that tiny sea creatures had crept into the space between the two moving parts preventing the movement which would have fired the fuse. With great reverence I popped those I could rescue back into the ocean with many heartfelt thanks!!!!

Mount Wise

During the clearance of unexploded devices on the foreshore at Torcross, my boss instructed me to demolish, with explosives, a concrete pill-box above the fresh water lake.

Torcross was one of the practice battle beaches used prior to the D Day landings. It was bombed by the Air Force, shelled by ships and the landing forces used live ammunition, including rocket propelled shells and grenades. It was generally an unpleasant job. Sometimes we found the results of casualties, which had to be buried. Foxes and other predators had been at work fortunately. The scaffolding on the beach below high water still had anti-boat mines attached and these proved difficult to remove. Several had either previously blown up during practice landings or come adrift and fallen on to the sand, subsequently being buried by the shifting sand. Many days were spent probing the sand for these mines and several were discovered, most without fuses.

The time came to demolish the pill-box. Before leaving Plymouth I took the precaution of telephoning the RAF Air Traffic Control to tell them that I would be making big explosions by demolishing pill-boxes at Torcross. I repeatedly asked if there were any over-flights planned for the area on that day and the Controller affirmed there were no flights scheduled anywhere in the area of Startpoint and Torcross.

I had already calculated the explosive charge formula for the thickness of the concrete construction. Soon after arrival, and after a brew-up of tea, the charges were laid. The idea was to lift off the roof, then with other charges slightly delayed blow down the walls. The concrete was reinforced with steel rods which I thought would cause the concrete to crack into small pieces. I decided to use slow burning fuses, one foot per minute. Everything was ready, nothing had been left to chance. Sentries were out at each end of the seaside road armed with a Very Light pistol and three green and red cartridges.

The road was a restricted area and no civilians were allowed within several miles but it was used by the military and some authorised civilians. When all was ready I intended to fire off one green flare to which both sentries would reply with a green flare. They knew that when the fuse was lit there would be a three minute delay before the big bang. I was standing on a high vantage point by a deep slit trench which had a steel roof over one end into which I would jump when ready to start the fuse. Making a thorough search of the whole area, down to the seaside road and out to sea, nothing moved. Firing the next red flare I jumped down into the trench and ignited the fuses. Three minutes to bang time. My senior rating counted down 70 seconds... 60 seconds... 50 seconds. It was then that I heard the sound of the heavy engines of a large aeroplane. I shot out of the trench and looked towards the sound of engines. Coming directly towards me just above sea level was the unmistakable shape of a Sunderland Flying Boat. It flew over the cliff and was over the pill-box just as it erupted with a very large bang. The roof sailed upwards in slow motion and I was forced to jump down into the trench under cover to avoid being peppered with fragments.

The Sunderland lurched and wobbled and seemed to be getting lower over the land. I climbed to my vantage point again to try and spot the plane, which I lost when it was hidden by a range of trees. Recalling the sentries I checked my handiwork and was pleased with the results of the charges.

With thoughts of a future court martial for blowing one of our own aircraft out of the sky, we packed our gear and headed for Plymouth. Arriving at the Bomb & Mine Disposal Office which was attached to the C in C's Plymouth Mount Wise headquarters there was a message to say that the C in C's aide wished to see me immediately. I was not allowed time to wash and brush up but went across to the 'holy of holies'. A Wren officer greeted me coolly and I had to wait half an hour before a door opened and a Commander RN bade me enter. With knocking knees I stood to attention. He simply told me I had to report to the Commander in Chief at 09.15 hrs to-morrow. As you may imagine, I did not get much sleep that night!

I was not helped by my fellow officers who had been given details of my plight by my boss. They had a field day. At 09.15 I attended as directed. Promptly on the appointed time I was ushered into the C in C's presence. He stood with his back to me looking at the coast chart in the Dartmouth, Salcombe, Torcross area. As he turned he said he understood that I was getting rid of pill-boxes using explosives. I agreed this was so. He paused then surprised me by saying, "Well done my boy, you are doing a grand job." He then apologised for getting me worried about the Sunderland. He explained that he had suddenly decided to fly along the coast to survey the battle ranges from the air and had ordered the pilot, instead of flying parallel to the beach to fly inland, hence the incident.

There were not many senior officers who would have been big enough to apologise to a very junior officer. The thought strikes me though, what would have happened if the plane had been brought down?

Target - Channel Islands

As the war in Europe drew to a close we were told we had to help to liberate "somewhere". Although it was secret we had an idea it was to be the Channel Islands. The word was that it could be a rather 'dodgy' operation as the garrison under General Rudolph Wulf had refused to surrender and was determined to fight. With this in mind we embarked on the Troopship HMS Ulsterman. The army personnel were none too happy at the idea of a sea journey and their discomfort was further enhanced by events which took place shortly after we had set sail.

We left Plymouth Harbour and the escorts were about three miles astern shepherding their charges into a manageable convoy. Checking with my No.1 Sub Lieut. Johnny N. that we had our three Royal Marines and all the equipment safely on board and finding everything in order I went onto the boat deck for a smoke and a breather.

In the distance I spotted what appeared to be two fast running Hunt class destroyers racing toward the convoy and there was an air of expectancy with the ship's company. Gun crew's were 'closed up' (a term meaning ready for action) and the two guns in line with the approaching ships were aiming their barrels toward them. The "Ulsterman" and the convoy zigzagged toward the setting sun and one of the escorts was making smoke. Suddenly the destroyers turned to starboard together and raced for the misty grey shoreline. Obviously something unusual was afoot.

Beside me several Army Officers stood apprehensively watching. Nearest me was a Major clearly very worried taking deep draws on his cigarette which his shaking hand barely held. Smiling I said "Looks as if we are going to have a moderate sea for the crossing". As he mumbled a quick "Hope so" there was an enormous explosion which momentarily deafened everyone. The destroyers had dropped a pattern of depth charges, the shock wave of which pounded the hull of the Ulsterman so that every plate rattled.

The Army Officers were more than anxious and I realised something would have to be done to reassure them so I told them the destroyers were on exercise, getting ready to go to the shallow waters of the Pacific where they would be hunting Jap subs. They accepted my story almost unanimously, the exception being the Major and he did not seem to be in control of himself, so I asked him to follow me and without questioning why or where, he did so. Out of hearing of his colleagues he told me this was his first trip on a ship and he had always had a dread of the sea. It was quite clear too that he was in the first stages of seasickness. Going down to the lower deck I got him to sit on a Carley float next to the water tight door marked WC Officers Only - it looked as though he might be needing it very soon!

In the Wardroom I introduced myself to the R.N. Lieutenant there and explained that some of the army officers were having anxious moments and asked if it would be possible to open up the Wardroom for drinks. After consultation with his superior the request was granted and the "medicine" soon calmed trouble nerves. As darkness fell the ship's tannoy ordered "Hands to darken ship" and the Army Officers were allocated dinner places in the Wardroom. I stayed in the company of the Major who, after three gin and tonics was feeling much better. We ate a pleasant if somewhat hasty meal.

The 'buzz' had got around that the German Commander of the Channel Islands was refusing to capitulate and he and his troops were going to fight to the death. Everywhere on the ship troops could be seen checking and cleaning their weapons, the few exceptions being those suffering the agonies of seasickness. The sick berth attendants of the Ulsterman and members of the Army Medical Corps were much in evidence caring for the victims.

By midnight most of the Army Officers were attempting to get some sleep in readiness for the dawn landing although some were checking that their troops knew the correct landing craft stations and the loading drill. Another Captain was cleaning and loading a Sten gun, another was busy writing a letter.

Going to the upper deck I found one of the ship's officers puffing away at a large hooded pipe and asked him about the activities of the two destroyers at the beginning of the journey. It seems that a U-Boat was thought to be trying to escape through the Channel to neutral Eire or Argentina and the Nazi captain had boasted that he intended to attack as many troop carrying landing craft as he could. There were 27 ships rushing in the same direction as ourselves.

All too quickly dawn broke and I said a prayer as we approached in the landing craft. Ahead was St. Helier and in the early morning mist a fort on high ground and the entrance to the harbour were visible. Behind me the Royal Marines were unfolding the Polish Mine Detector and getting two reels of white tape ready to mark the area as it was cleared of mines.

Twice the Beachmaster, who was travelling with us, ordered everyone, including officers, to keep their heads down in case there were snipers about. A large stone breakwater came into view on our left. Thankfully it appeared unoccupied which was just as well because an enemy with a machine gun could have caused many casualties on our side of the craft.

We turned quickly to starboard as the engine suddenly reduced speed and the blunt bow dropped a foot or so. At the same time the Beachmaster's voice came over the loudhailer "Stand-by" and almost immediately followed by "Go", the landing craft touched bottom with a jerk that sent some who were unprepared sprawling and as we grounded so a machine gun opened up in short bursts. The ramp dropped and I followed a much practiced drill. Taking the earphones from the marine I put them on and replaced my tin hat. I took the mine detector and stepped down the ramp onto the mud of St. Helier Marina. The two Royal Marines were behind with the reels of tape, some short metal rods and a bundle of red metal hoops with a metal cross in the centre. Switching on the detector I received an immediate signal and wherever the detector was placed it gave a positive signal.

Meanwhile the troops still in the landing craft remained "heads down". Taking another step forward I kicked something in the muddy water. Upon investigation it turned out to be a heavy chain and it was obvious that with so much metal around the detector could not possibly work. Looking around it was also very clear that between the landing craft and the sea wall, some thirty feet away, there were miscellaneous ships chains, old anchors, wires and, most important, the whole muddy area was covered in recently made footprints! It was evidently quite safe to go ahead so with the tapes making a ten foot wide corridor I returned to the landing craft to give the "all clear".

My next, very pleasant, duty was to escort Commander Piroquet to the Town Hall. Picking up his brief case he stood for a moment to survey the scene and, at that instant, the sun shone, brightening the whole harbour area. Great tears filled his eyes and ran down his cheeks. "Lieutenant," he muttered "I've waited years for this." I answered "Let's go, Sir. You're home once more", which was all I could manage before tears filled my eyes.

The Commander, with me as escort, walked across the mud and up the jetty steps to the road above. We were not aware of any noise apart from occasional small arms fire in the distance. As we reached the top we replaced our tin hats with our naval caps and then a massive cheer went up from the people lining the road, hitherto unseen by us. The Commander was instantly recognised and enough tears of gratitude flowed to fill many buckets in the time it took to reach the Pomme d'Or Hotel where the German Naval Headquarters were. It was quite clear to me that the Commander was in safe hands so he agreed that I could leave him and get on with the next assignment, which was to render safe all explosives in the harbour area to allow the much needed food ships to dock as soon as possible.

My hair started to go grey shortly afterwards for I had to deal with a booby trapped weapon store and a 'rank' happy Major who almost blew up St. Helier docks.

Saturday May 12th. Three L.C.A. (Landing Craft Assault) beached at St. Helier Harbour.

Another mine rendered safe at Dungeness, 1945

Rendering a mine safe, 1945

The Day St. Helier Nearly Blew Up

A priority was given to the clearance of enemy explosive devices and weapons which may have prevented the docking of Allied Supply ships into St. Helier harbour. On landing day plus one, although the Army had arranged guards at the quay head a small child had stepped onto an explosive device and received severe leg injuries. When we heard about this my party and I thoroughly investigated each jetty warehouse. When the Germans surrendered, their small arms were to be placed at specially defined storage places. We approached each warehouse with extreme caution going through the drill of seeking out booby-traps and having made everything safe we entered this particular warehouse to discover the biggest cache of explosives and weapons we had ever seen and I was horrified to see, on the concrete floor, hundreds of shining detonators strewn everywhere.

Piled high on the right were hundreds of rifles, machine guns and pistols. They lay where they had fallen, a hotch potch of barrels and stocks, and further investigation revealed that mingled with them were dozens of German stick grenades. Whoever had placed them there had made many into booby traps by removing the caps of the firing strings and wrapping the pull strings round trigger guards. One tug and then there would have been a short delay before the grenade exploded. Sympathetic detonation would have been most likely since close to the piles of rifles, etc, were several depth charges of an unusual but highly sensitive type. On the other side of a narrow gangway were torpedo war heads and more depth charges. It seemed that the child's injury must have been caused by treading on a detonator.

The Army was approached and the guard doubled on this highly dangerous store, thus keeping out all personnel without an authority card issued by me. Whilst near the Pom d'Or Hotel we decided to try and eat our 'K' rations for at this time we were still without food, the supply ships being unable to land much needed rations until the area was safe. The gallant St. Helians were themselves severely short of food.

Our efforts to cook with the materials issued were doomed to total failure but fortunately we had plenty of cigarettes which staved off the worst of the hunger pains. Continuing with our task of making safe, Johnny Norton took one jetty and I another. As I approached the guard at the jetty head he saluted and at the same time the distinct sound of a pistol shot came from the weapons store. I rushed forward drawing my pistol, not really knowing what to expect. As I ran toward the open door I could see the tell-tale gun smoke creeping out through the door. The scene that met my eyes was of the soldier who had been on guard outside the door in company with a very cleanly dressed (as compared to all of us) Army Major who had in his hand a small German Automatic pistol.

It transpired that the Major had just landed on the jetty and noticed the soldier on guard and demanded to know what was going on. He then looked through the window saw the pile of weapons and took particular interest in several small automatic pistols lying in amongst the rifles. Going in, he was fortunate that he did not tread on a detonator and that the pistol he choose was not attached to one of the booby-traps. Having picked up his new toy, without checking to see if it was loaded he pulled the trigger, whereupon several small bore bullets sped off and on their way hitting the firing mechanism on top of a depth charge of which, fortunately for everyone, the cords were not pulled out to their fullest extent. If they had been I should not be telling this story now! The resultant explosion would have been devastating for the whole of that part of St. Helier not to mention the loss of life.

The incident was reported to the Senior Army Commander and disciplinary action no doubt took place, for it appears that the major had been told that the warehouses were out of bounds for all personnel without an official pass. But he had pulled rank on the sentry and threatened all sorts of disciplinary action if the soldier did not stand aside, so he stood aside!

Jersey, Channel Islands

St. Helier harbour entrance had been mined and the German Mining Lieutenant would not reveal what type of mine had been laid or where. He protested that he did not know, but after a little 'gentle persuasion' he showed us some maps and lists but could not give much information. (Many years later I discovered he had not long been in Jersey so really did not know much about the lay-out).

The diving launch in the charge of an elderly warrant officer arrived and a 'professional' seaman diver was sent down to search for mines. If he found one he was to return to the surface and I would go down and attempt to render it safe so that the type could be analysed. Whilst one diver is down working another is almost fully dressed for diving. All he has to put on is his helmet and then he is able to quickly assist if needed.

Another diver attends to the lines which connect the diver to the boat. Both lines are armoured and will stand almost anything before damage occurs. One is the air line and the other a telephone which, in my experience, never worked so you rarely attempted to use it!

After thirty minutes or so in about forty feet of water, the diver signalled that he had located something. He was called up to the surface and described his find. At this point the wind was increasing and the sea getting very rough. The warrant officer called a halt and markers were dropped around the spot and we had to return to the quay.

The next day, although the sea was still rough, the wind was less strong. We managed to find the spot and the diver located the object. When he returned to the boat he made his report and my attendant finished attaching the rest of the equipment. I went below and found the object some nine feet in diameter made of an alloy lying on a sandy base.

In order to be absolutely sure which type of firing mechanism it was I had to put my hand under the mine. Whilst I was doing this in the disturbed sandy bottom I felt something grab my wrist. All divers fear conger eels and I thought that was what had grabbed me, and was afraid to look in case my hand was no longer intact. It took me a while but in the end I plucked up the courage to look and saw violent movement around the base and thank goodness I had the required number of fingers.

It did not take long to discover all I needed to know about the mine and I was taking stock when a pull on the lines from above told me to return to the surface which I did, still unsure what had grabbed my hand. Up above, once again the weather was deteriorating and the sea too rough to continue so we ran for safety to the harbour.

Having landed I was walking along the quay when a messenger arrived to say that a mine was found some mile or so off-shore on rocks. The only way to reach this mine was by water so we commissioned a local fisherman to take us round. The seaman diver was with me and, as we approached the mine site, he asked if there were octopus in the area.

Our fisherman's answer was "Yes" and he added that before the war when fisherman caught octopus in their nets they turned them inside out to keep them alive and still until they returned to harbour where they would sell them to the foreign chefs from the holiday hotels. So it was very possible that what had grabbed my wrist could have been an octopus. Not a very pleasant sensation I can assure you.

During the occupation civilians were not allowed on the beaches but the moment the Germans capitulated children naturally wanted to play in the sea and on the beaches. It was reported that a group of under 12 year olds were on a beach to the eastwards which, a hurried glance at my map told me, was heavily laid with anti-tank 'Teller' mines. With all haste I gathered my party and our mine detector and went to the danger area. The Police and Army had already cleared the immediate area and had strung warning notices along the entire frontage and promenade.

We had no difficulty locating our first half dozen mines. These were some 100 yards on the sand along the foreshore and were easily rendered safe. They were very corroded and, therefore, I decided to explode them on site. A rock about house height would serve well to make any blast wave go to sea without damage to the foreshore houses. I stacked my mines at the foot of the rock alongside a natural cave of about three feet in depth. We retired to the landward side posting sentries and establishing that all was ready to detonate. A slow-burning fuse was cut, a detonator cramped on and placed snugly into the prepared PBG charges alongside our Teller mines.

Exactly to the second the air was rent by a gigantic explosion, much larger than expected. The whole earth shook and a lump of rock at the highest point was dislodged and fell. Out of the corner of my eye I saw it falling and with a mighty push I sent my Sub-Lieutenant flying but not before the edge of the boulder caught him a glancing blow on the shoulder. He went down as if poleaxed and the rock embedded itself in the sand nearby.

Johnny was a tough one though and before long he was on his feet ready to carry on and, apart from some hefty bruises, nothing was broken and no real damage done. It was at this point that a elderly gentleman (about 40 which seemed elderly to us at 21 or thereabouts) came trotting toward us, cursing like mad and with shaking fist proceeded to inform us that all the time the Germans were in charge no damage had occurred and now we b***** British had arrived and only five days at that, we had knocked out every window for miles around! It seems about 32 panes of glass had been broken or cracked on various properties running from the shoreline inland about an eighth of a mile. Needless to say there had to be the inevitable Court of Enquiry.

The Army eventually arrived to assess the claims and duly settled with those claimants, after which the experts of geology came along and completely exonerated me; it seems that my rock which I had used as a detonating place stood on a strata of deep limestone which ran in a narrow seam from out to sea inland for a quarter of a mile, which made an excellent shock wave carrier!

There was also another factor of which I was unaware. The Germans had concealed a large quantity of explosives in the base of the rock which could be detonated by a switch from a cable laid into the rock under the sand. It had been cemented in and the years of immersion by the tide had covered the area with seaweed and marine growth which successfully camouflaged it. It was not my lucky day!!!

Bombs "On the Rocks"

The weather was sometimes too rough for diving operations so other tasks were carried out as there was much to do. The Bomb & Mine Disposal Party had been very busy since our arrival and on this particular day we were setting out to do some clearing of beaches, etc. when a report came in that a fisherman had seen an unexploded torpedo or mine to the east of St Helier. The object was on the rocks. We contacted the fisherman and he offered to take us to the site but we would have to wait until low water as the 'whatever' was covered by a normal tide for about half an hour.

The next day we set sail in the fishing launch. I had with me the minimum of equipment plus a few demolition charges. When we arrived at the site we landed, in company with the fisherman's dog, and climbed over seaweed covered rocks until we came to the object which I quickly identified as a 1000 lb American bomb and a look at the fuse told me it was a time delay type. The only thing to do was to detonate this bomb. It was so far off shore that its effect would not be felt there. Leaving me behind with my demolition gear the crew plus the fisherman went out to sea in order to watch the explosion from afar.

Working quickly, for I knew that the tide would be sweeping in very shortly, I scraped off the barnacles and weed around the fuse pocket, laid on four pounds of polar blasting gelatine, placed the detonator with a minute and half slow burning safety fuse, and tamped my charge with nice grey shiny clay.

Climbing on the highest rock I surveyed the area. There was not a sign of life except my crew lying off about half a mile away waving to me. I had already decided on my cover which was a natural cleft in the rock about 2 feet wide and about 4 feet deep approximately 50 yards away. Back at the bomb I checked that the fuse was 1½ minutes and lit it. I fired one red Very light and scampered over the rocks to my place of safety. Twice I stumbled and once got my foot wedged in rocks. I had just got to my cover and slipped off my bag of explosives and bent below the edge of the rock when the detonation took place. Great lumps of rock went sky-wards, hot pieces of steel and stone fell uncomfortably near but the bomb had been disposed of.

After all the 'missiles' had finished falling I picked up my bag and retraced my steps to where the bomb had been, this was to make certain that the whole thing had been completely destroyed as sometimes there is a partial detonation leaving exposed and dangerous explosives.

Waving to the crew who were cruising toward me, I approached the spot where the bomb had been and could see a large crater some 15-20 feet across, grey mud and clay had been thrown for over 50 yards and the rocks nearby were covered with it. A few more steps and I was looking into the crater. What I saw nearly sent me into a panic for there on the side of the crater was ANOTHER BOMB. The fuse on this one was severely damaged and if like its mate it was a delay action type then it may already be working. I waved frantically for the fisherman to bear off and after a moment's hesitation, he gathered something was amiss.

With the tide rapidly approaching I quickly prepared another charge and attached it as before but this time I gave myself two minutes to get away before detonation.

Once again a scan of the horizon, everything clear so repeat with the red Very light, and lighting the fuse I once again scrambled over the now very slippery rocks. A quick look at my watch told me I had been on the move a minute. It was my intention to get further away but the going was tougher than I anticipated.   Happily I reached my cleft in the rock and had a look to see the state of the incoming tide. My watch showed another half minute to detonation.

The flash just 50 yards away followed by an enormous rush of wind then a bang caught me unprepared. I dropped to the ground and the earth seemed to shake. Lumps of rock screamed through the air and a black smoke screen covered the area in which I sheltered. For a second or two I lay there shaking like a leaf then I shouted because I thought I was deaf but I heard it and knew I was OK. Picking myself up and collecting my bag from where it had fallen, I walked slowly over the rocks to look at the scene. This time, although the crater had extended considerably there was no sign of a bomb for which I said a fervent prayer.

A movement in a pool of water nearby caught my eye. A fish was turning over and over in a thrashing frenzy. It rested for a moment then swam away into deeper water as the gulls, which had been absent, flew over expecting a feast, only to be disappointed. In a short while the incoming tide broke over the mud between the rocks to seaward then a wave rushed through several rocks and a spout of water like a waterfall dropped into the crater and in a few moments the crater was full and I realised it was time I was out of there!

The launch approached and the fisherman gave me instructions which I followed. I had to climb over a good few hundred yards of slippery rocks before they were able to pick me up.

At the very moment of the first detonation, my assistant Johnny N took a photograph of it from out at sea. I took a quick photo of the second bomb in the crater..... Why two bombs? Subsequently I discovered that an American Marauder bomber was attacked by the very effective flak ships steaming just outside St. Helier harbour and in order to get away quickly it jettisoned its load of two bombs. It was said to be flying just above sea level at the time of release, which probably accounts for the fact that neither exploded.

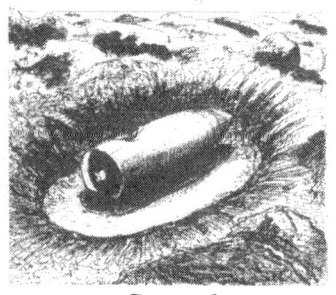

No.1

Second

It was a good thing the second bomb did not detonate at the same time as the first one otherwise I do not think I would be telling this story now!

Was There a Body in the Bag???

Lots of rumours were circulating about the enemy who were said to be laying boobytraps under dead bodies and anything else to cause havoc during their retreat. Such was the thought of the finder of an object in the surf on the beach at St. Helier, Jersey, C.I.

A constable had spotted it and had summoned help. They were sure that the 'thing' was a dead body enshrouded in canvas. It couldn't be left where it was so they carted it to the nearest mortuary. At about 9 p.m. I was told that a booby trapped corpse had been found. I scrounged a large glass of whisky from somewhere and went to collect my tool kit. The constable took me to the mortuary, the first time I had ever been in one, but it was just as I had imagined. On one wall a bank of metal drawers or doors, the lighting was poor and in the middle of a damp floor stood a pedestal sink-like table about 8 feet in length and 3 feet wide. Water oozed from the object lying there and it trickled musically down a pipe into a metal gridded gully. The smell was awful. I felt sick and wished I hadn't had so much Scotch. When I think back on that day even now I get a decidedly queasy feeling.

What WAS in the bag? For there it was, a canvas shroud some seven feet by three feet and the body shape was very obvious with the head appearing to be looking over the right shoulder. There seemed to be a large chest and at the other end its feet were also large.

Using my torch I scrutinised every smelly inch for a more careful inspection but not a mark did I find. Furthermore any telltale signs of a booby trap escaped my notice. The nagging thought was that my corpse and shroud were upside down and anything which may have helped was underneath. Suddenly, aware that I was entirely alone, I felt like running out, but courage returned and sanity told me that canvas could be cut. I selected my very sharp double sided divers knife and made a quick incision on the left corner by the back of the head. A horrible squashy repulsive liquid covered my hand and knife. I rushed, retching, over to a tap and let the water pour over me and the knife.

I knew I would have to take decisive action so I returned to the slab and rapidly cut through the canvas some twelve inches across the corner toward the top of the head. It was my intention to ascertain if the corpse had an identity tag so with rolled shirt sleeve and tie less I prepared myself. (In those days rubber gloves were not available therefore my hands were unencumbered).

Not daring to stop and think about it my hand went quickly into the opening and as I thrust my arm deeper; out of the opening came foul reddish brown gunge. I dared not look, so averting my gaze I explored with my hand toward the neck area - something was not right - I could feel no jawbone, surprise caused me to look once more at my corpse and as I did so the raised chest area suddenly collapsed into a hollow accompanied by a gush of dreadful smelly air.

It was then I knew that there was "No body in the bag" as what came out clutched in my hand was a soaking mess of kapok, a cotton thread like material commonly used as filling for boat cushions and mattresses. In seconds my knife laid open the complete bag - no corpse - no booby traps - just a mattress from a sunken ship. I cleaned myself up, washed my knife and was violently sick! I stumbled out into the yard and was greeted by the constable.

He was kindness itself. I don't know where he got it from but he insisted that I drank brandy - lots of it. I can't remember much after that, but next day the following appeared in the local paper!

There was no "Body in the Bag"

About 10.30 on Saturday a First Tower resident was walking along the promenade when he saw a long green canvas bag on the beach. He went down to it and came to the conclusion that the bag which was about 8ft long and 2ft wide might contain a body, so he informed Cenatuer J de Brun of St Helier, who lives nearby.

Police were sent out with the ambulance and the bag was taken to the General Hospital Mortuary where it was opened and found to contain not a body but Kapok Down, gravel and sea weed. The bag was examined by a Naval Officer at the request of the police and was identified as a life saving float as used in HM ships.

The Magpie Syndrome

St. Ouens Bay was used as a collection point for German explosives stored on the Island and tons were carted there by the Army every day. All crates were neatly stacked and the whole area was well guarded, but souvenir hunters are like magpies. They cannot resist picking up odd and sometimes strange objects. Many a British household still sports war relics from the 1914 - 18 war and beyond, brought home by servicemen to remind them of their experiences.

Grenades being relatively small seemed to take the fancy of many. With this in mind I realised that the boxes and boxes of French Egg Grenades would be coveted by the compulsive collectors, so I emptied 20 grenades of their powder explosives and withdrew the firing detonator. This made them much lighter and they looked the same but were then harmless. I made it known to the Army Sergeant in charge that if his working party wanted a French Grenade souvenir, they could get a safe one from me. Many of the work party approached us and by the end of the first day 15 grenades had been issued.

The next day I had been working out Hexanite explosives from German torpedo heads which was very heavy tiring work so I decided to take a breather. Some 400 yards away an army truck stopped alongside some crates containing the French grenades. A soldier came into view and it seemed as though his hand snaked into one of the crates. At first I thought I was mistaken, then it was obvious that he was going through the motions of unscrewing the detonator and firing unit from the body of the grenade, then emptying the explosive powder onto the ground.

His next action rendered me voiceless. He held the whole detonator firmly in his left hand and with his right hand quickly pulled out the safety pin. The grenade handle flew into the air and still the soldier held firmly onto the detonator unit.

Desperately I started running toward him shouting to him to drop it in the open space behind the truck. Jumping over explosive obstacles I had not gone very far when there was a vicious crack and quite a lot of smoke. When the smoke cleared I had almost reached him. He just stood there looking in a surprised manner at the place where his fingers once joined his hand! After the ambulance had left it was discovered that the soldier had already been issued with two of the safe grenades to take home with him so why he felt the need for another heaven knows, but his actions made him disabled for the rest of his life.

End of Bachelor Days

In the autumn of 1944 with a bunch of officers I was invited to a dance at a Wrens' quarters. We duly arrived and one of the first people I saw was a blonde Wren whose name I discovered was Brenda. We danced almost every dance and arranged to meet again. We met in and around Plymouth but could not go to a lot of places as I was a commissioned officer and Brenda a rating (a boat's crew wren). She could not come to the Officer's Club and I could not go to the NAAFI canteen, which made our courtship a bit difficult.

Two months after that first meeting we became engaged and a wedding was being organised for May 29th, 1945 when orders suddenly arrived to report for duty somewhere overseas. The general opinion was that it would be the liberation of the Channel Islands. The "powers that be" promised me I would be allowed to fly home for the wedding so arrangements went ahead, the precious cake was ordered, ham cooked and scarce things which had been hoarded for such occasions were unearthed, only for me to be told the week before the wedding that I could not be spared. Pandemonium reigned at the home of the bride. She of course was out of all the panic, still on duty as a boat's crew wren in Plymouth.

Cancellations were sent out, the cake although made had not been iced so it was put in store, but two lots of guests who could not be contacted in time, turned up! However, after two eventful months in Jersey (more of which later) I was able to return home for our wedding on July 9th, 1945.

Return to HMS Volcano

After our wedding in July 1945 we returned to Plymouth and I received orders to report to HMS Volcano (where I had trained in Bomb and Mine Disposal so long before) for a six weeks course on Japanese underwater weapons. The war in Europe was, of course, over but the war in Japan had not then ended. Brenda was able to get unpaid leave and accompany me. We stayed in a hotel in Seascale for a few days until we found lodgings on the sea front. She had to leave Cumberland (as it then was) before me to return to Plymouth as her leave had expired.

Soon after my course finished I was posted to Dover and Brenda was demobbed from the WRNS. She quickly joined me in Dover, where we found a super flat (after six weeks in an awful one) and had a very happy time there.

I was very surprised to find how much my eyesight had been affected by using binoculars and periscopes earlier in the war and this became most noticeable when searching for mines on dark beaches, usually in howling gales and torrential rain. The mines were often in the surf and very difficult to spot. Many times after walking a long way from the nearest road I missed the mine as did my crew which resulted in lost time and energy. We carried an Aldis lamp but even with this aid we had many a search.

A local fisherman told us "Two miles walking on these beaches is equivalent to five on the road" and it certainly felt like it. One particular evening when Brenda and I were having a quiet evening listening to the radio the Duty Staff Officer telephoned to say a mine had been reported to the east of Jury's Gap and it was expected to beach at Dungeness. So I changed into my work gear, warm clothes and sea boots ready for the task ahead. Brenda persuaded me to allow her to come with us rather than sit at home wondering what was happening. She donned her Wren uniform and joined us on the mission.

Strictly speaking she had no right to wear the uniform or to be in Naval transport but we had not been married very long and she was very persuasive (also there had been one occasion when I had left home at 8.30 am. and was not seen or heard of again until 11.30 pm. She was in rather a state when I did get back). There was a bonus in having her with us. It turned out she could spot a mine in the surf from quite a distance saving us miles of trudging. She came with us several times with the N.O.I.C Dover doing a "Nelson" until he was officially informed and he had to decree she was not to come anymore. This was a great shame as she not only saw the mines quickly for us, she also carried the heavy Aldis lamp and battery!!

The Channel Tunnel - 1945

The gales in the Channel were abating but this did not mean less work for us. Once again the duty officer interrupted my dinner. "Sorry Bombs" he said, "There's a mine washing ashore under Shakespeare Cliffs alongside the Channel Tunnel workings and its a priority job." Without more ado I changed into my working gear and collected my crew who had already been alerted.

Bomb and mine disposal people had a special arrangement with the local railway management. All rail traffic had to stop through the tunnels whilst a mine was threatening and in order to speed up the process of dealing with it they would provide a locomotive which would take us to the nearest point. Dropping us they would beat a hasty retreat back to Dover station yard.

Now came the hard part as the only way to where the mine had been reported was down the cliff face - with ropes. When we arrived at the tunnel workings it was, of course, still raining. In about 10 minutes with the help of our Aldis lamp we had spotted our mine. It was jammed between the rocks and by the look of it had been well and truly pounded by the gigantic waves breaking over this rocky part of the coast.

It was a British mine and very dented and I felt certain the bashing it had taken would surely have torn its insides to pieces. I had however to go through the normal rendering safe procedures as stranger things have happened in the past and I could not take any chances. The mooring wire was still attached, about twenty feet of it spread between various rocks. Apart from being scratched the mooring switch was in the off position, most horns were badly twisted and one was missing. The special 'C' spanner would not fit because of damage to the castellated slots so I had to use a cold chisel and with a few practised strokes managed to release the security ring which came away without any more difficulty leaving the main bung.

Using a lever I tried to prise it upwards and out of its seating so that access to the detonator would be possible. Twice it almost came out but then remained stubbornly in place held by a rubber sealing ring. Once more I tried then, in exasperation, put the torch down and, trying to keep my cigarettes dry, managed to take one out and light it. After four or five puffs it spluttered out at which, cursing the weather, I threw the sodden remains onto the beach.

Leaving the torch at my feet I selected a larger lever and with much grunting managed to prise the bung upwards. It came away and I dropped it alongside the torch. My right hand groped into the 4 inch cavity. Nothing - but there should have been!?

As I bent to pick up the torch for a closer inspection suddenly night turned into day. I was rooted to the spot completely deaf and blind, I thought I was dead. In a while I felt able to reach around for the mine. When I located it the thing was still intact and I was in a tight spot and my crew didn't know what to do. They were at the recommended safe distance from the working. After 5 minutes - which seemed more like hours - I found a rock and shakily sat down. The rain beat incessantly on my face and rivulets ran uncomfortably down my back inside my shirt. Now I was sure I had survived. Heaven couldn't be so uncomfortable nor Hell so cold*!*

It transpired that after cleaning the threads of the bung, a switch wire had touched the cleaned threads and made a circuit which fired the detonator. Fortunately for me, in its passage across the rough ground, as I had suspected when I first saw the condition of the casing, everything inside had been torn loose and the detonator housing had come adrift from the main explosives thereby saving my life.

Three hours later, after climbing back up the cliff face we were obliged to walk through the railway tunnel to the harbour beach, over the railway line to the Lord Warden Hotel which had been taken over as Naval quarters. It was one very relieved and thankful "Bombs" who returned to the mess!

The Channel Tunnel Explanation

Whilst searching for the reported mine at the base of the cliff, my Aldis lamp beam shone on a massive steel door on the face of the cliff. It was about 30ft wide and 20ft high and its centre joint was welded together. I was totally mystified but hadn't time to ponder. The next day I learned from the police that what I had seen was the entrance to the exploratory workings of what was to be the Channel Tunnel, started in 1822!

Hastings Harbour

March gales were blowing with great strength in the Channel and many ships were forced to run for shelter in the nearest port, and fishermen along the south coast were unable to leave their harbours.

It was in such conditions that I received a call from the Duty Staff Officer. "Bombs," he said "A mine has arrived in the middle of the Hastings fishing harbour. It's been there for three days and, as the gales should be easing, the fishermen want to get out to sea as soon as possible. Please make it a priority as the fisher folk are getting rowdy." I gathered my crew from their barracks and, by the time we were ready to leave, our 5 ton truck arrived complete with red flag flying.

It took almost 2 hours travelling before we drove into the fishing harbour to the east of Hastings. Fishing boats large and small were poised ready to slip across the beach into the heavy waves. There, about a quarter of a mile off the beach and almost centre of the harbour, was a very large many horned mine, which I could identify as being British. It had not moved since it was first seen three days before so it had evidently trailed a long length of its mooring cable, which, almost certainly had fouled some underwater obstruction. This posed quite a few problems so to relieve the situation I resolved to borrow a boat to go round the mine at a distance of about 50 yards, floating a light hemp rope around the mine to form a lasso. The plan then was to tow the mine away to the east under the cliffs at Fairlight Glen.

Getting the rope posed no problem at all but getting the loan of a boat did! No one would let me have a motor boat so I had to plead for the use of a strong rowing boat. Eventually I was given a heavy ex-ship's lifeboat. Two of my crew were willing to row. With reluctant help from the fishermen we managed to get the boat launched through the surf through to the breaking waves and off we rowed. By this time all soaked to the skin. We had rowed almost half way to the mine when one of the crew warned me that a fisherman was shouting and waving a large piece of paper. Reluctantly we turned the boat and headed for the beach.

As we went through the breakers and surf we were once again soaked to the skin. When we grounded I jumped over the side and approached the senior fisherman expecting him to give me a signal from Dover telling me to go to another mine that had greater priority. NOT SO ! What I was greeted with was "Now Sir, that be my boat you have there. Will you sign this ere bit o paper to say that if you blows up my boat the Admiralty will give me another ?"

Normally I do not swear but I gave him all the swear words I could bring to mind !!**??* Returning to the boat we took off for the mine once more with my crew working like possessed men. That way they managed to work off some of their fury.

The good news is that three sea sick making hours later the troublesome mine had been towed ashore and rendered safe. Towards dusk we got back to the fishing harbour and handed over, all in one piece, the boat and rope to its owner.

Just as we were about to leave for Dover the senior fisherman came up to us. He shook hands with all and taking me aside, and pointing towards a large fish and chip shop on the promenade, said "See that? It belongs to me and when you and your crew come this way at any time you can have fish & chips and a pint of beer, free of charge, on me." I thanked him and we all went for supper then, very good it was too. We returned several times thereafter and always had wonderful treatment. "He wasn't such a bad old so and so after all" exclaimed my crew.

1914 - 1918 Mine

On one occasion I received a telephoned reprimand from a Senior Admiralty Officer for telling a newspaper reporter that mines would be around, picked up by fishing nets or washed ashore for years to come. I was forbidden to speak to the press, very odd as not many weeks before this I had been told that as censorship had been relaxed I was to give support to the National Press.

It seems that during a busy period when I had rendered safe 57 mines in three days and nights, one member of press asked if these types of sea mines would come ashore or menace shipping in years to come. I told him it was more than likely as not all mines laid had been recorded accurately. Bearing in mind that around the shallow waters of the world some 300,000 mines were laid, 30,000 of these around our coasts and enemy occupied coasts, and there is no knowing how many of these blew up, broke adrift and were rendered safe or how many are still on sea beds.

Ten days after my reprimand I was called to a mine which had washed ashore north of Margate near a sanatorium. It had been laid during the 1914 - 1918 war and was covered with barnacles and oil, its horns were bent and active but, although I treated it with a great deal of respect, it was not difficult to deal with. Internally it was perfect, which says a lot for the British workmanship at that time. The serial number indicated that it was made in Sheffield.

One question springs to mind.... where had that mine been all those years?

Dredger - Dover Harbour

It was called "Empire Mammoth" and it was a very large and dirty dredger and was engaged in the task of clearing the sea bed between the harbour entrance and the dock, a job it had been busy on for several days. Tons of silt came up in the many buckets which was then tipped into a barge alongside. A winchman saw it first and quickly gave the alarm, for to his horror, there was a very large bomb in one of the buckets. Clanking machinery stopped immediately, the crew flew a large red flag from the masthead and promptly piled into a launch to abandoned ship.

At this particular time I was practising rendering safe on an earlier recovered German Magnetic mine. To make my efforts more realistic my Petty Officer had laid a booby trap and if I 'fell' for it a small bang would let me know where my mistake was. All was going well and I had almost completed the rendering safe procedure when the telephone rang.

The call was for me from the Duty Staff Officer reporting that the dredger in the harbour had picked up a bomb in one of its buckets. All cross channel ferries and other shipping movements had been prohibited and the nearest buildings were evacuated. It was to be given maximum priority.

Gathering my tools and crew we drove to the harbour jetty where a small tug took us aboard and quickly delivered me alongside the dredger. After getting my tools and myself on the dredger the tug, with my crew, sped away and out to a mooring half a mile away. Steam was spraying from various pipes and joints, groans and bangs came from all directions and the wind had freshened making the dredger roll uncomfortably.

There was little time to dwell on the circumstances for there, four feet or so above the deck was my problem, a 1000 pound German bomb, wedged in one of the buckets. The fuses were situated in the side of the bomb, one near the nose and the other near where the tail joined it. The tail unit had sheared off when the bomb hit the water and was probably under the dredger and quite harmless. Unfortunately for me the fuses were on the lower side of the bomb, making it impossible for me to see them and it was imperative that I determined the type with which I had to deal. They could have very sensitive tremblers, although I doubted this considering the rough ride from the sea bed to where the bomb now rested. It could have one nasty 17b clockwork fuse which may already be ticking away. This thought caused me to get my stethoscope (doctor type) from my tool bag. I fitted the ear pieces and stepping onto a girder placed the other end on the nose of the bomb. By this time the dredger was rolling quite badly with its anchor and dredge lines taut which all added noise to an already noisy vessel.

With difficulty I strained to listen and to my horror heard a steady ticking. To make certain which fuse carried the clock I moved rapidly but unsteadily along to the other end of the bomb, placing my stethoscope as near as I could to the fuse and was amazed at what came through to my now, very sensitive hearing. The ticking was if anything louder and at that moment missed a beat or two.

Was this the end, had my time run out? Then just as I was going to move the ticking started quite evenly again. I was relieved but perplexed, I had never heard of a bomb which had two clocks fitted. Logic told me it could not be so unless the German armourer had made a big mistake when fusing the bomb prior to being loaded onto the bomber.

The next task was to somehow carefully revolve the bomb so that the fuse heads would be exposed, with luck I would be able to read the fuse numbers on its head. If one number had 17b on it, that would be the one with the clockwork timer. Stepping down on the deck I searched around for a strong length of metal to use as a lever. I wished I knew how to use the steam crane. It would have been so much easier to lift the bomb with it and then turn it, but that was out of the question. Lady Luck had not deserted me however as I almost fell over a four foot long crowbar. It was pretty unwieldly but I soon placed it carefully under the bomb and, using the leverage and exerting my efforts, the bomb gradually turned an inch or so.

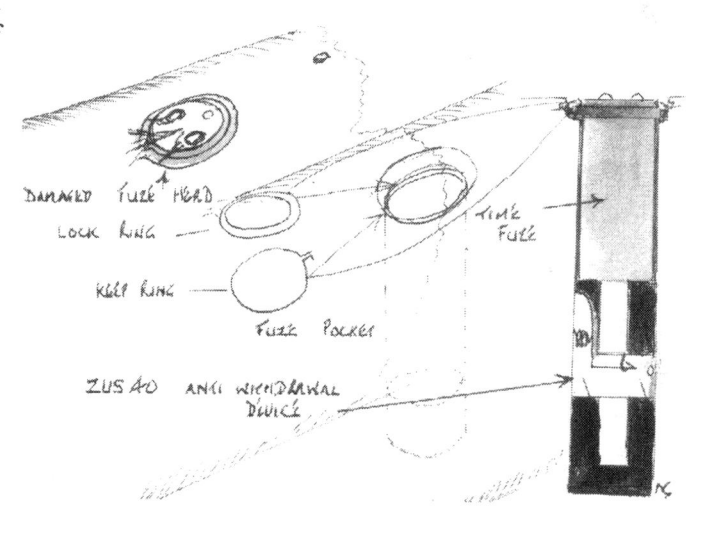

After a lot of perspiration and energy loss I could at last see the fuse heads. Both were covered in a mixture of mud and sea water for the bomb was, fortunately for me, resting on a soft cushion of mud which is probably why it was relatively easy to move. What wouldn't I have done at that moment for a nice cup of tea or a gin and tonic. I contemplated browsing in the below deck galley to see if there was something to drink, even water would do, but dismissed the idea. I would do what had to be done to this bomb first. With a rag, both areas of the bomb fuses were cleaned and dried.

The sea was getting even rougher and movement on board was extremely uncomfortable. Two long hours had passed since I came aboard. On went the stethoscope and, wherever the business end of it was placed, the ticking was steady, rhythmic and equal in density. This perplexed me more than ever so hanging my stethoscope on a convenient hook my intention was to step down onto the deck, do some brain storming and hope to come up with a solution. Just as I started to move a particularly rough sea rolled around the dredger and as she heeled over I pitched backwards a few feet against a steel structure. Putting my hands behind me to protect myself I grabbed a three inch pipe. We were steady again for a few moments and my senses were alerted most forcibly for the pipe I had grabbed was a very hot steam pipe. It was whilst I was rubbing my sore hands that I heard it again, but much louder, the ticking which had been puzzling me so much. The cause? Well, when the crew abandoned ship they shut down the boilers and the steam pipes were ticking during cooling, the noise evidently being conducted through metal to the dredger bucket and to my bomb!! I felt rather stupid and resolved not to tell a soul.

Back to the bomb. One fuse was so badly damaged I had to use plasticine to build around the head to enable me to pump in a benzene fluid which would collapse the fuse and, hopefully, destroy its electrics. The second fuse was also damaged so I was unable to be certain of the type. The number certainly ended with a 7 plus an undecipherable mark near it. Accordingly I treated it as if it were a clockwork 17b. The plan was, hopefully, after the fuses had been rendered safe they would be gently removed.

One fact in my mind was that several army disposal chaps had been killed whilst removing already treated German fuses. It was obvious that booby traps had been introduced for it seems that the bombs had exploded when the fuses were almost withdrawn. A short while before 'my bomb' we had been advised that the Germans had introduced an anti withdraw device. This went under the code of ZUS 40.

When I withdrew my fuses I mentally kept my fingers crossed. The first one came free and was carefully placed in a box and I peered down into the fuse tube - nothing was there. On to the other one which might have a clock. This fuse was difficult and was sticking but I managed to get a pair of grips onto it when it was an inch out and prised it up a fraction at a time. Quite suddenly it was free and was in my hand. It had a beautiful but ruined clock. I placed it in a box until I could remove its detonator and then, with the aid of my pen torch, looked down the fuse tube where, to my horror, I could see a shiny metal device which I recognised from the drawings sent from HQ as a ZUS 40 just waiting for its spring to rush across its hammer to strike an igniter to blow up the bomb. Very rapidly I mixed a small quantity of plaster of paris and carefully ran it down to gag this monster.

If there had been a Guinness Book of Records for the fastest gagging of a firing device, I would surely have won it! Quickly my tools were partly cleaned and placed in the tool box, the fuses were made safe and put into safe containers. Looking at my watch I discovered I had been busy for almost six hours. The tug answered my signal and quickly came alongside the dredger. The dredger crew returned and operated the crane to lift 'our bomb' on to the tug to take it ashore for subsequent disposal.

Returning to my office I made out umpteen reports, had lashings of tea and a few ship's biscuits. The Petty Officer reminded me that I hadn't completed practice on rendering safe the rigged German Magnetic mine so I got down to it. I had only a few more moves to make and once more I could claim "a clear round." One more wire to unclip ---- bang - I failed. What a different story it would have been if it had happened on the dredger! Going back to the Officers Quarters near the Castle I had a luke warm bath and was ready for a nice cool gin and tonic.

Next day I had a message to say 'well done' from the Dover base Captain but no word of thanks from the Harbour Board or the dredger owners. Wouldn't it have been terrific if I could have claimed salvage money?

DREDGER FINDS 1000lb. BOMB.

The Empire Mammoth, which is engaged in the dredging of the Harbour brought a 1000lb. bomb to the surface in one of its buckets on Monday afternoon. Members of the R.N. Mine Disposal Unit, which is stationed at the Dockyard, were summoned, and identifying it as a German blast 500 k.g. bomb, rendered it safe. It was placed in the dredger's cutter and brought to the Eastern Arm on Tuesday morning, when the crew of the Disposal Unit had it hauled ashore by crane and took it to their Headquarters where it will eventually be dismantled.

The bomb, thought because of its type to have been dropped by enemy aircraft during the early raids on Dover, contains about 500lbs. of amatol and T.N.T. It is 4ft. 9ins. long and fitted for aiming with a tail which would have brought its over-all length to 6ft. 6ins. Its diameter is one and a half feet. The tail of this type of bomb is attached by means of aluminium fittings which shear on impact, when the electrically controlled fuse is set in motion.

Dungeness 1945

It was very late when the duty officer came into the wardroom bar at the "Lord Warden" and over to me. Having a few minutes to spare I was catching up with the news in the paper. "Sorry Bombs," he said "the coastguard at Dungeness reports a large mine ashore about half a mile west of the lighthouse." Going quickly to my cabin I changed into working rig. The truck with my crew arrived fifteen minutes later.

Gales had been blowing for the last three days had not abated so we had a rough ride from Dover. The civilian driver took us to the nearest road to where 'our mine' was reckoned to be. It was pitch black and the time was two a.m. Gathering my mine disposal tools and the Aldis lamp (which had a very strong beam) I started walking along the waters edge toward Dungeness. On the landward side at the top of the beach stood miles and miles of scaffolding which was intended to delay an enemy landing. Waves were crashing onto the beach and I was beginning to get wet from the spray blown from the sea. As usual, the exhausting task of walking on a pebble beach (one step forward, two back) was beginning to take its toll. After about twenty minutes slogging along, the beam of the lamp picked out the mine.

Approaching, I was able to identify it as a large German 'Y' Type. It shouldn't cause undue problems for I knew them exceedingly well as by this time I had rendered safe 55 over the past few months. This one was lying a few yards from the incoming tide.

Obviously it had been deposited on the beach at the previous high tide which meant that the report I had received had been a late one. However, it was clear I would have to work very fast to beat the tide so to start with I quickly gathered from a pile of debris on the foreshore six short pieces of planking. To render this mine safe it was necessary to remove the detonator from its base which of course was resting among the pebbles. To get at the detonator I scraped the pebbles away from the base until there was a hole about a foot deep then placing some of the planks there made the mine steady.

Things were progressing well and in twenty minutes or so the mine was steady and unable to roll. Underneath it I excavated more stones and the hole was now deep enough for me to get my head, shoulders and forearms into. With all speed I undid the detonator securing nut at the same time getting very wet from the tide (which was being driven by an ever increasing wind) pouring into my hole. Still I was used to getting wet.

I was very pleased when the detonator came free, this meant that the mine was almost safe. It was at that moment that a rogue wave came up the beach with great force and broke over the top of the mine and in so doing washed away my carefully placed pieces of wood. The whole weight of the mine (approximately 1000 lbs.) rolled onto me in the water filled hole. I had to gulp air whenever the water allowed it.

It seemed the more I struggled the less body movement I had and waves were coming at a greater force and frequency. The nearest help was too far away to hear any distress calls. (The crew must never be in the danger area). It was more and more obvious that if I didn't get free soon the tide would drown me before it was deep enough to float the mine off my body. It was then I did what I think others would do in such circumstances. I Prayed.

Although a choir boy in my youth I could not claim to be a church goer. However I did consider myself a Christian in thought and deed and quite enjoyed Naval church services. Given the predicament I now faced with the sea water almost covering me, I gulped in air and prayed, "Please God help me get free." Three or four times I pleaded, then a great flash of white light occurred and I was able to push the mine off me as if it was an air balloon. Scrambling to my feet I found that the detonator was still in my left hand.

After a while I located my soaking wet hat, bag of tools and lamp. Within a quarter of an hour the rendering safe procedure had been completed. The Aldis lamp was down at the waters edge and it still worked so I flashed a signal to my crew and they acknowledged. It was while I was wringing out my socks, etc., waiting for the crew to arrive that what had happened came into focus. There was no thunder or lightening about, so what was the intense light? how did I manage to raise such a weight from myself? There are no answers - but that is what happened.

Before the crew reached me I did say 'Thank you' many times. The safe mine was rolled up the beach and secured firmly to the scaffolding until it was removed to the mine 'graveyard' in Dover Docks to join all its mates that had been rendered safe over the past few months. I later scrutinised my German 'Y' type for any peculiarities - there were none!

Penny-Wise!

"The police have just come through with a job, Bombs. There's a mine washed ashore at Cooden and its urgent. They've evacuated the area and cordoned it off." So the message was presented to me by the Duty Staff Officer. The problem for me was we had a merry party in progress in the wardroom to celebrate the demobilisation of one of the long serving officers at the Dover base. Yours truly had consumed a few glasses of cheer but such a message always alerted me instantly.

Within 20 minutes my truck arrived complete with my crew of two seamen. The time was 10.40 p.m. The civilian driver had been with me several times and knew that I expected a fast run to the destination. This non stop run was no exception and we passed through quiet villages and coastal towns. Arriving at Hastings we picked up a police escort who took us along the shore road to within a quarter of a mile from where the mine was reported to be. Shortly we came to barriers which prevented entry of traffic. The barrier was moved and we proceeded towards the promenade. About three hundred yards from the sea front the flashing light from a Police sergeant brought us to a stop. The sergeant and I had met on several occasions and I had recently accepted the splendid hospitality of the local police at their canteen after attending other mines in their area. "Its down on the beach, not far from the steps from the promenade" he directed. "Its a hell of a big one, in the first instance it was report by the beach Superintendent."

Collecting my bag of tools from the truck I started walking toward the sea front. On my left was a large empty brick built hotel, its garden behind a wall was very overgrown. By the time I got to the corner I could see the spray from the rough sea breaking near the promenade and the wind was still blowing at almost gale force.

Quite suddenly I was aware of my protesting bladder. I turned and went back towards my friendly police sergeant "I'm afraid I must have a wee" I told him. "There's no loo here" he said, "but go into the garden, its overgrown and you can do no harm" was his welcome advice. I did just that and felt much more comfortable as a result.

Picking up my tool bag I passed my police officer friend and told him I wouldn't be long and continued walking toward the corner. All I had to do was cross the promenade road, down the steps and I would be where they said the mine was lying. If it was, as they said, a really big one I guessed it would be a German 'Y' type. Anyway I would soon know.

I was not more than 20 feet from the promenade when with a terrific flash the mine exploded. The bang deafened me and the flash blinded me. For several seconds I wondered if I was still in one piece or even on this earth. Fortunately the five foot high garden wall on my left had shielded me from the blast. All I had to contend with was the falling roof tiles, and tons of pebbles and sand from the beach. Surprisingly I sustained no injuries. It did not take long for me to realise I had just had a lucky escape. The moral of this incident - if nature calls - heed it !!!

A Lobster's Catch

The call came from the Dungeness Coastguard that a fisherman had picked up something in his nets which he had dumped near to his mooring in Rye Harbour. It was marked by a red buoy and at ebb tide in two hours time would be high and dry.

We travelled to Dungeness by truck and arrived almost at low water and the sea was getting rough. There near the piles the red buoy was still afloat. Gulls swooped over me as I walked along the muddy foreshore. One obviously disliked me intensely for it dived down like a Stuka Dive Bomber and as it pulled out of its dive something came from it and I felt the thing slap onto my cap. I took it off and there it was, white and wet. I thought, "What a good thing cows don't fly". The thing on my cap looked like the perfect shape of a lucky black cat - only this was white.

The red marker float was touching bottom so I waded into the sea. A few waves broke and sent water up and over into my boots. Shortly after I was able to grasp the rope securing the buoy to the heavy object. As I gently pulled on the rope I could feel it tighten, with water covering occasionally I could still see that the object was the remains of a German explosive float. It was tangled in the fisherman's net. Further along was a yellow metal cylinder which turned out to be a 5 gallon drum. I pulled in the slack net but the oil drum made a very effective anchor.

The tide was ebbing fast and I could see the oil drum had been cut off leaving a jagged edge. Inside as it lay on the sand, almost halfway in, something moved. Taking one of my 'rending safe' levers I prodded the sand carefully. It felt as if the lever had been grasped by an unseen hand. Pulling on the lever there was quite a weight. Giving an extra pull the lever suddenly came out with a very large lobster still grasping it. The more I tried to release its hold on the lever the more it resisted.

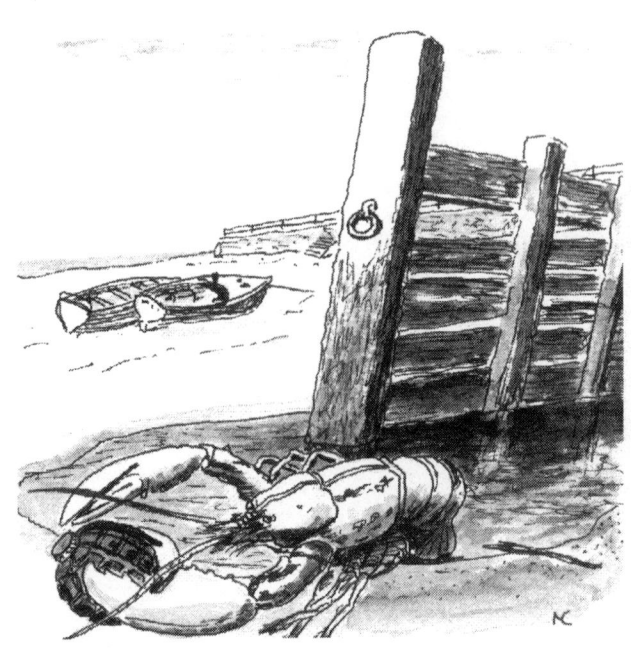

The huge creature gripped the lever with its left claw, the other claw held what appeared to be a stone covered in seaweed. Taking a strong hold on the lever with both hands I started to swing the heavy lobster toward high water mark. At the end of a mighty arc, the lobster let go and dropped into a pool near the groyne.

The stone it was gripping fell off and rolled along the sand where it glistened in the weak sunlight and its covering of seaweed fell off. I walked over to it wondering why the lobster had taken such a fancy to it. What I saw I couldn't believe so squatting down to get a closer look I could see it was a Mills Hand Grenade. Gently rolling it over so that the part which held the firing lever was visible I could see the safety pin was missing and the lever had sprung at least an inch from the body. A closer look indicated that it was stopped by a .38 bullet which was jammed between the lever and safety pin axle. If the lever had moved an inch it should have exploded.

Quickly I assessed the options. I could attempt removal of the bullet, push the lever back and put in a safety pin, but it may have exploded so the best thing was the course I took. Building a high sand mound I placed the grenade alongside some PBG (Polar Blasting Gelignite) and blew the grenade up successfully. Having got rid of this menace I made safe the German explosive float, pulled in the rest of the fishing net and released many crabs, one small lobster and a sole back to the sea. The net was later returned to its owner.

Disappointment followed for I had intended taking the lobster back to Dover for a meal in the Officers Mess but search as I might there was no sign of my anticipated meal. Since then I have seen many lobsters in fishmongers shops, but none as large as 'my catch'.

MINE NEAR MAIN STREET

Safety men worked with a searchlight

Evening Standard Reporter

A coastguard at Sandgate, at the western end of Folkestone, saw a mine shortly after midnight near the sea wall—about 100 yards from the main street with its houses and shops.

Police went from house to house rousing sleeping families and advising them to evacuate, and a message was sent to the Mines Disposal Squad at Dover.

The mines squad found that the mine was very close to a groyne, with which it threatened to come into collision.

It was secured with a rope and then, as coastguards shone a searchlight on the mine, the Navy men made it harmless.

And Sandgate was safe again.

Pluto

Pluto, the pipeline terminal at Littlestone on Sea was a busy place during and after 'D' day. Its remains had not been cleared and many lengths of pipeline were lying around the place. Several concrete roads had been made near the foreshore. leading to the high water mark where they were used by vehicles with pipe laying equipment.

We had been busy rendering safe mines which had been washed ashore along the coast. The last was at Dungeness and it was raining very hard when we commenced the drive back to Dover. We were all hungry and knew we would be too late to get any food at the naval base. With this in mind I decided we would go to the pub at Littlestone where we asked for pies or sandwiches. Although they had nothing the landlady went to her friendly butcher and came back with a goodly supply from which she produced delicious food for us. Whether or not she had used their week's rations I don't know but we were extremely grateful and, saying our farewells to these hospitable folk, resumed our journey in a much happier frame of mind.

The vehicle we were in was a 15 cwt van with windows around and seating for six or so bodies. I was driving, the rain was still pouring down and it was pitch black. In those days headlights had to be masked, the light was emitted through a tin like contraption fitted over the headlight with a cross some two inches long each way and about a ¼" gap. Not much light managed to escape this device and its a wonder the roads weren't littered with wrecked military vehicles and masses of bodies. Amazingly they were not!

Driving out of the pub forecourt I turned right and then right again onto the concrete road leading to the main road which hugged the foreshore. Several cross-roads had to be passed and having negotiated these we were running smoothly, or rather the Ford van was, at about 35 mph. The windscreen wipers were less than efficient and I was peering through the rain swept screen at the straight road ahead, when suddenly the wet surface changed colour and texture. It was then that the 'penny dropped'.

What I was looking at was the shingle on the foreshore road down to the sea. I braked hard sending my crew forward to strike one another from behind, at the same time wrenching the wheel to the left. There was a sloppy noise as the tyres slid on the concrete in a sideways skid. We dropped a few inches and turned 90° from our original course. Almost in slow motion we came to a halt. At the same time the vehicle turned gently onto its side, my side. Fortunately the detonator and other explosive boxes held firm but the crew collapsed behind me. Amazingly no-one was hurt. I instinctively switched off the engine and we were plunged into darkness. All was quiet - expect for the rain which still poured relentlessly down.

I instructed our tallest member, Kim, to stand carefully and open the nearside door which was above his head, which he managed splendidly. Kim helped all to de-bus then he had to evacuate himself and, in so doing, caused the only damage in the whole episode.

Levering himself out he accidentally put his foot on one of the windows which promptly cracked. We surveyed our 'wreck' and came to the conclusion there were enough of us to push the vehicle onto its wheels, which, with a few huffs and puffs we did and, apart from the cracked glass, it was unscathed.

We re-boarded and drove (carefully) back to Dover without any further happenings. In the morning I reported the incident to the Transport Officer who ranted and raved like a person possessed. He suggested that we had been joyriding and that the vehicle would have to be out of service for a day to have the cracked glass replaced. Furthermore he would report the matter to the Naval Officer in Charge. The man was a fool, of which the Navy had its fair share. One thing I did know was, whilst we were working in the rain and cold at Dungeness, coping with unexploded mines, he had been in a nice warm, safe bed. Incidentally, I heard no more of the incident so NOIC Dover must have known that we really were on duty.

SEA MINE WASHED ASHORE

Beach Cleared And Parade Roped Off

Soon after mid-day on Thursday a number of holiday-makers on the beach at a point opposite the Sackville Hotel on the East Parade had a scare when they were told by police car loud speaker to leave immediately as a sea mine was washing ashore. It was first seen by the coastguard on duty at the Colonnade watch house drifting east.

He notified the police.

As soon as it became evident where it was likely to wash up, Mr. H. E. Delaney, the borough parade inspector, went to the East Parade and warned those who were on the beach and walking in the neighbourhood. Chief Inspector R. V. Nice came in the police car and an announcement was made over the loud speaker, telling the people in the houses facing the sea to go into their back rooms and to leave their windows open. The area was roped off and warning notices put out.

The Parade Inspector watched the mine wash nearer to the beach. He saw it bump over some rocks and strike a groyne before it was washed up and came to rest. There were some anxious moments before the receding tide left it high and dry some 20 yards from the sea wall of the parade at about one o'clock.

It was a mine of British origin, which had evidently been in the sea for a considerable time, as it was thickly encrusted with barnacles.

The danger area remained roped off until a party from a Mine Disposal School, under Lieutenant Cashford, R.N.V.R., arrived about 7.30 in the evening and in half an hour rendered the mine harmless.

Considerable blast damage was done to the Sackville Hotel and adjoining property, and window glass over a wide area of Bexhill was broken, when a mine came ashore and exploded on the beach there about two years ago.

Civic Reception ~ Hastings

During the time I spent in Dover I travelled many times to the Sussex and Kent coastal towns. We rendered safe, in the Hastings area in one long week, 29 mines of various origins; German including magnetic, one acoustic, one French Saute Harle and umpteen British Mk 17s and 20s.

Before we arrived on the scene some six mines had blown-up causing an awful lot of damage to property on the sea front. It was as a result of our efforts over Christmas 1945 that we were invited to a Civic Reception at Hastings. This included a visit to the theatre for the pantomime where my crew and I were writhing in our seats with embarrassment when the principal boy sang 'Hearts of Oaks' specially for us!!

Needless to say we had an extremely good afternoon and evening. I'm always pleased to open the photograph album at this section, not only because of the memories but.... I had a good head of hair then.

Later, when the hotels and guest houses had managed to refurbish and get started on their season, Brenda and I were given a free weekend which we thoroughly enjoyed.

MAYOR'S PARLOUR
TOWN HALL
HASTINGS

16th January, 1946.

Dear Lieut. Cashford,

As some slight recognition of the debt that the town owes to you and to your brave fellows, in dealing with the danger from floating mines, I should very much like to have the pleasure of entertaining you and your men to lunch on Saturday next the 19th instant.

I thought perhaps if you could call here, at the Town Hall, at about 12.45., we could then go on to lunch, spend the afternoon at a very jolly Pantomime which is now playing at the White Rock Pavilion, and finish up the party with tea.

I am sure you would receive a very hearty welcome from the people of the Borough.

I am sorry that the notice is so short, and I should be glad if you could let me know by 'phone, Hastings 4182, whether you can give us the pleasure of your company. I do not know what arrangements you would make for getting across here, but if it entailed any expense, we should be pleased to meet it.

Yours very sincerely,

Mayor.

Lieut. N. Cashford, R.N.V.R.,
    B and M.D. Officer,
        Staff of Naval Officer in Charge,
            DOVER.

Littlestone on Sea

After an unusually quiet period the inevitable call came from the Duty Staff Officer saying two objects, believed to be mines, were washing ashore, one at Littlestone on Sea and the other at Winchelsea. My crew collected the special tools and the truck plus civilian driver. This time instead of taking my smaller vehicle I travelled in the cab. The police at Folkestone and Hythe provided motor cycle escort through the towns.

Leaving New Romney we continued along the coastal road toward Littlestone. The tide was coming in and a black object could be seen about a hundred yards beyond the anti-landing craft scaffolding barrier which ran as far as the eye could see parallel with the foreshore.

Inland holiday bungalows and houses had their windows open with curtains flapping in the breeze in order to minimise the risk of damage should an explosion occur. Through the binoculars I could see the object was a German 'Y' type mine and estimated that it would be against the scaffolding in half an hour. The tide would be high in about ten minutes and, taking due consideration of the strong winds blowing from the sea, the mine would be high and dry ready for my attention in about one hour.

Sending the crew and driver into New Romney for a snack I sat, with my bag of special tools for German mines and a length of light rope. The day was pleasant despite the strong wind. I sat amongst the grass and sand dunes on the foreshore. As I gazed at the houses and bungalows opposite I noticed a silver haired gentleman working in the front of a small detached house. The windows, unlike most of the houses around, were closed. Getting up I stuck a red flag on a pole near my tools and walked across the road.

It was apparent that this gentleman, engrossed in rubbing down paintwork on a window sill, was hard of hearing as he did not know I was near until I was about five paces away. He turned, smiled and greeted me. I explained what I was about to do and recommended he opened all windows to limit damage should there be an explosion. He hurried to carry out my recommendation. On his return we chatted. He had retired ten years earlier, was bombed out of two houses in London and had been at Littlestone six months. I judged him to be seventy at least. "When you've done" he promised "I'll make us a cup of tea", an offer which I gratefully accepted.

Returning to my red flag and tools I once more settled down to wait. The mine was still about ten feet from the scaffolding and had floated to eastward. Hopefully it would be driven by the wind through a gap in the scaffolding caused by a previous mine exploding against it a year before. It was quite amazing for, as I watched through the binoculars, the mine raced toward the gap, its speed was uncanny. Quite clearly there was a natural tide race in that area, possibly caused by scouring and small sand banks between the open sea and the barrier. The mine had a few more yards to go and I estimated that it was in about five to six feet of rushing water.

Coming to the gap it stopped for a moment then rushed through. By then I was standing watching in wonder, without binoculars. The mine disappeared through the water race in the gap and came to the surface seeming to leap out of the spray.

The whole of my vision then was taken by a sudden bright light which rapidly turned to yellow then red. My heart came into my mouth and there was an ear splitting explosion, the sky and the near seascape was blotted out by tons of wet sand, sea and thick black smoke which billowed upwards in a mushroomed shape cloud.

The blast threw me backwards, my cap fell off and was carried across the road. Getting to my feet I realised I was uninjured (thank you Guardian Angel). I could hear the echo of the explosion for several seconds running along the coast. In minutes the cloud of smoke and bits and pieces settled although for some time masses of debris fell sizzling and steaming into the sea and on the foreshore where white hot metal landed. The gap in the scaffolding was large enough now to get a fair sized ship through. Only twisted metal poles and pieces of German mine lay in the gap.

When the tide went out souvenir hunters descended on the immediate area. They didn't find anything of any value as I had collected ten fair size flat fish and one good cod and these were given to the locals. The silver haired gentleman was the first to run to see if I had been injured. He kept his promise and provided a pot of tea which was more than welcome. One of the neighbours came with a bottle of gin which he pressed into my hands in gratitude.

As I walked to my tool bag and the still flying red flag, reflecting that I had done all I could, the truck came round the corner and stopped beside me. "Whilst we were having our tea there was a hell of a big bang from inland" the driver said. "I reckon the army were doing training at Brookland". "Could be", I said and started loading the tools and flag into the back of the truck.

Despite a strong wind blowing from the sea and a spectacular explosion less than a quarter of a mile from the nearest house, not one window was cracked or broken and the only casualties were a few fish.

The Mine Disposal Unit which is responsible for the coastline between Hastings and Broadstairs, have rendered safe 700 mines and ten bombs since 1939, (something like 540 tons of explosives). 225 of the mines have been dealt with since VJ-Day. This small unit's personnel are Lieut. N. Cashford, M.B.E., whose home is at Tunbridge Wells, P.O. B. Judkins, A.B. R. G. Turner, a former Barton Rd. schoolboy, who lives at Ivy Cottage, Temple Ewell, A.B. Crowder and A.B. Roberts.

With nothing more to do we travelled on to Winchelsea to deal with the mine there. This mine was under the cliffs which went along the coast to Hastings. It was rendered safe without too many difficulties, the main charge was removed and the TNT exposed by removal of the filler caps followed by the usual procedure for burning out the explosive. This time though it took four attempts to get the fire going. After three minutes or so the main explosive started to burn. Soon the heat was so intense that it was inadvisable to stand within ten yards.

The crew went off on the usual search for tea. I got behind a groyne as dense clouds of black smoke poured across the foreshore toward Dungeness Point. The sentries had done their work well and no people were in the danger area.

After twenty minutes and much smoke and heat the fire was out. 800 lbs of a very highly explosive device had been reduced to a harmless pile of twisted metal and soot.

WINTER HARVEST OF THE SEA

All through the winter gales, when mines were being washed up along the South Coast, the mine disposal units were hard at work. Today the harmless weapons are stacked in rows at Dover docks.

The New Romney Mystery

The saying that "all is not as it seems" was very true on one occasion when I was called to an unexploded bomb in the garden of an empty house at New Romney. Mines, not bombs were my speciality so I was less than pleased to have this one to deal with. It seems the Army were engaged elsewhere so could not attend. After loading the truck with the UXB tools we drove to Romney arriving almost an hour later.

A barrier across the entrance to a road proclaimed "STOP - NO ENTRY - UNEXPLODED BOMB". A Police officer came from one of the houses nearby which were occupied mainly by the Army and said they were all evacuated and then led me to where the bomb had been found. There it was, ten paces from the rear of a large house, in soft ground beside a wide concrete path which led to a glassless greenhouse. I was extremely surprised to see the bomb so near the surface. By its diameter it would be a 50Kg. After the police left I took stock of the situation and several things worried me. The end of the bomb was above ground by an inch or so and it was slightly off the perpendicular. At this trajectory it must have come off the roof so I went down the overgrown garden and peered up but could see no sign of damage to the roof. Getting on my knees on the path to closely examine the bomb and the path edge I could see the path was heavily scored and by scraping the soil gently from the side of the bomb I could see deep scratches in the metal indicating it must have dropped close to the path edge, which caused it to wobble out of its true line, hence the odd angle.

Just as I started clearing the soil which covered the bulk of the flat end of the bomb one of my crew shouted to say a mine had washed ashore along the coast and was to be given priority. Hurriedly leaving, assuring all concerned that I would be back before nightfall we proceeded along the coast to the beached mine which proved to be a French one. It was awkward to deal with but eventually it was made safe and we all returned to New Romsey arriving there whilst it was still daylight.

During the return journey I had gone over in my mind what had been done so far and what facts had been established. It was then I realised one major piece of evidence had not been inspected; in amongst overgrown roses and gooseberry bushes were several pieces of rusty metal. Arriving at the scene and after being severely molested by the bushes a battered conical piece of metal was extracted. Its widest part was about the right dimensions for the base of a bomb but it was too badly crushed to check its shape and size. It certainly resembled a bomb tail unit and my Petty Officer was convinced so he left me to continue my investigations.

Clearing the soil from the sides of the bomb was essential to try to ascertain what kind of fuse was fitted so I continued digging using mostly my hands. It was beginning to get dark and I had already spent three hours on this object. Eventually I felt what I thought was the edge of the fuse head on the side away from the concrete path. This was lucky as it meant the position was accessible for the tools needed to render safe.

Feeling much happier, my mind was jogging over the types of fuse likely to be found and which method of rendering safe would have to be employed, as I removed soil hoping to uncover the fuse head more fully when to my fury the sides caved in filling my carefully dug hole.

To give my aching knees a rest I partly stood up and in so doing stumbled and, trying to save myself, my hand came sharply into contact with the end of the bomb where my fingers found a round pencil like protrusion some 12 inches long surrounded by hard packed soil. Using a screwdriver with utmost care I removed the soil and found the pin was coming out of a larger diameter raised area. The steel pin had a few fine threads on its end. Never had I seen a German bomb like this so it was vital that the type of fuse was determined at once as it could be another of "Adolph's secret weapons" which had fallen into our hands. Being very careful not to bump or disturb the bomb I removed as much soil as possible. As it was now dark I went to the truck to get the Aldis lamp, not a soul was about - my crew had disappeared into thin air!!

Back at my bomb and with the help of the Aldis lamp I could see into the deep hole and by lying on my stomach could reach down to where the fuse should be. There was a slightly raised oval shape on which, by wiping away the dirt, I could see some lettering. Gingerly I rubbed some more and the oval shape suddenly slid away into the bottom of the hole.

To say my heart jumped several beats is an understatement. It practically stopped. When nothing else happened I managed to retrieve the piece from its resting place. Looking at it carefully and although it was upside down the words Qualcast Roller/Mower were clearly visible but I was still not sure so I excavated more soil from around my "bomb" until it was free whereupon I gave a good heave and it came away from the edge of the path. There it was painfully obvious that my "bomb" was nothing more than a dismantled lawn mower's roller!!! Clearly it had been out of service for a very long time but how it got into that position I shall never know.

Taking the tools to the truck, (my crew were still nowhere to be seen), I collected the canvas sheet used for carrying awkward objects. I carefully covered the "bomb" and tied the sheeting securely in place. When my crew returned - they had been royally entertained by a friendly retired publican and his wife - they lifted the object with great care into the truck wedging it with chocks against the wheel arches to prevent any movement.

When the police and army personnel came back wanting to know if it was a 1000 pounder, "No" I said "just over 100lbs", "I knew it was" said the army Captain. How could I disillusion them, or for that matter admit that I had spent many hours rendering safe a grass roller? They wouldn't have believed me, would they?

Fisherman's Surprise Catch

A mine had been picked up in the net of a Folkestone fishing trawler. When it came to the surface in the net the crew rapidly reversed the capstan and lowered it back into the depths. They then wisely placed a dan buoy to mark the spot.

On the point of contacting Chatham to arrange collection of a frogman diving suit, in walked a New Zealand Sub Lt. RNVR. We had both been on a course early in the previous year. Since then he had been doing superb work clearing the French Channel docks and ports of demolition explosives which the Germans had planted upon evacuation. Sub. Lt. H had been on leave in London and was in Dover to supervise the loading of new diving equipment onto the cross channel ferry. It didn't take me long to suggest he unpack diving suits and gear for both of us to use to deal with the mine in the net trawled by the fishermen. He quickly agreed and an appropriate signal was sent to his boss Lt. Cdr. G in Le Havre.

The formality to get crates opened to borrow some of the contents was frustrating. Even HM Customs were involved; you would have thought we wanted to use the gear for fun - bureaucracy has always existed it seems.

The New Zealander was an experienced and competent diver of the Special Port Clearance Team and although I was, strictly speaking, his senior as a Lieutenant I duly left the selection of equipment to him. In any case some parts of the equipment were new to me having been greatly improved since my last diving course 18 months earlier.

Very quickly the Sub. had assembled his gear. He wouldn't assemble the second suit and reminded me that he was the expert, which I was obliged to acknowledge. Leaving him to complete his task I went to arrange a harbour tug to take us from Dover to a point near Folkestone where the mine lay in its buoy marked fishing net.

Before loading the diving gear I asked the Sub. if he had checked that the new air bottles were full. This time he almost burst a blood vessel with anger and said if I wanted him to do this job he would expect me to have confidence in him. He again reminded me that he was an expert diver with quite an impressive record of diving hours to his credit.

Two hours later with a freshening south westerly blowing we arrived at our destination under the cliffs to the east of Folkestone. The Sub. had dressed whilst en route. Seeing that he had not attached a lifeline to himself I went to the bow of the pitching tug, obtained a coil of light rope and went aft. As I reached out to offer the rope to the diver he almost pushed me over the side in anger at this interference and I realised I had a tough guy to deal with.

Now the first thing a diver should do on entering the water is to open his air bottle control to check that all is well with the complete gear. Should anything go wrong the lifeline is to stop the diver drifting away and make recovery possible. Not so with the Sub. for he stepped onto the gunwale and without waiting for the stern to drop into the next trough, off he jumped. There was an almighty splash and in seconds he had disappeared close to the rudder and propellers (which of course were stopped). Both my crew and I searched the roughening sea but there was no sign of the Sub. Lt. To say I was worried was an understatement.

He had been down without trace for over a minute. Tying the lifeline round my waist I stepped onto the gunwale and down on to the rubbing strake (a ledge which runs round ships hulls), crouching down so that I could see under the vessel. At that moment an extra large wave raised the tugs stern revealing the top of the propellers and an area of the ship's bottom. It was then I saw a hand and arm protruding from the bilge keel but no other movement. I knew that some pretty quick action was needed and grabbing a long boat hook instructed my crew to pay out my lifeline.

I reached down, kneeling, and with both hands holding the boat hook I steered it down to where the hand had been, felt something and pulled hard. The tug dipped into another wave trough and the stern came out of the water and at that moment I gave a great heave on the boat hook and a lifeless body came out. The hook had caught lightly round the air tube from the air bottle. Leaning over I managed to grab the exposed hand and pulled. Two crew members and one of the tug's crew grabbed parts of the rubber suit and between us, with much exertion managed to heave him onto the deck. Tearing off the face mask I saw that the Sub. was blue and lifeless. Turning him gently we applied artificial respiration. To our surprise and delight a murmur came from him and in a few moments he was moving freely and within a further minute or two he sat up against the bulkhead and sipped a cup of hot sweet tea.

The tug meanwhile raced back to Dover where the doctor proclaimed no damage had occurred to the Sub. Lt. so off he went on the train to London to a lady he had met on the first day of his leave.

Next morning he turned up promptly at 08.00. This time he obtained six more air bottles from his crate of diving gear but this time, before attaching for use he weighed them and carried out the test procedure as laid down in HM manual! The lesson he learned the day before was that because he considered himself the 'expert' he had developed considerable complacency and had not bothered to check that his life giving air bottle was full (the one used the day before was empty).

We went off in our tug in the afternoon and this time the Sub allowed me to attach a lifeline and act as his controller. The operation was successful and two hours after entering the water he was back on board and the tug was a quarter of a mile away from where the mine was buoyed. My demolition charge had been laid on the mine and at the expected time the sea erupted, a column of water shot 30 ft skywards followed by a dull metallic thump. The tug returned to the scene and her crew picked up a quantity of stunned cod. I imagine fish was on the menu in their homes that evening. The New Zealander rushed off to London to his lady friend and I went back to make my reports.

Next day Sub. Lt. H returned, and supervised the loading of his diving stores onto the ferry. He returned to have lunch with me and just as he left, gripped my hand in a firm handshake and simply said, "Thanks". I knew he meant it.

He returned to Le Havre and under the Lt. Cdr. RNR did excellent and very dangerous work around the French ports and finally on to Holland. I often wonder what happened to him after the war and if he made it safely back to New Zealand.

St. Margaret's Bay

Having washed, shaved and dressed I repaired to the wardroom for breakfast. The usual small talk flowed around me as I drank my third cup of coffee. A Wren Petty Officer arrived at my side with a message, it said that a mine was washing ashore at St. Margaret's Bay almost alongside the luxury house belonging to Noel Coward. Finishing my coffee I then asked the Duty Officer to alert my crew who, at that time, would be in the barracks, also the truck with the crew to pick me up in 20 minutes. I had already phoned the police and advised them to arrange for all windows in the vicinity to be opened and everyone to keep away from the windows facing the sea.

On arrival we descended the cleft in the cliff down to the bay. The local constable had blocked off the road with the customary 'Danger - Unexploded Bomb' barrier and donned his steel helmet. He indicated that the mine was out of sight under the cliff. The tide was still flooding and would be high water in about half an hour. Pulling on my wellingtons and duffel coat I proceeded to climb down to the foreshore over several very large rocks at the foot of the cliff, hoping to see the mine in order to identify make, etc., so as to select the correct tools. It required a hard scramble of some 70 yards over many more rocks before the mine could be seen. It had landed at the base of the cliff in a small sandy area enclosed by rocks. The sea occasionally broke over the rocks and ran up the beach and around the mine which turned out to be of British origin.

The horns glistened and the whole thing was covered in thick black crude oil! I clambered back the way I had come, by which time my first foot prints in the sand between the rocks had been obliterated by the waves. After collecting the tools required I retraced my steps. Reaching the large rocks which had to be climbed over, I rested a moment and gazed out to sea, several seagulls were zooming around something in the water. As I started to surmount the rocks a wave, larger than the rest, pounded my rock and broke casting a few feet of cold grey water around me. I was wet up to my thighs, my boots full of freezing water so I had to stop to empty them, squeeze out my socks and trouser legs and put them on again. To my amazement they were not uncomfortable. At this point I took off my watch and got out a small packet which I always kept in the wooden detonator box which travelled with the tools. Removing the circular white rubber ring I extended it, placed my watch inside and tied the end into a light knot and placed the whole thing in my jacket pocket. Even if I was to become immersed in sea water my precious 7/6d watch wouldn't get wet. I don't think Mr Durex ever envisaged his products being used for such a purpose!!

The mine was of little problem (apart from the oil) once I had removed the hand hole cover which gave access to remove the wires to the detonator. It was a problem then because of distortion of the threads. At some time the mine had received a very large impact across the top between the horns. Whatever hit it had had a very lucky escape.

After being made safe it was obvious the mine was unrecoverable, so the top and bottom plates would have to be removed which meant unscrewing dozens of nuts and bolts. My crew joined me to help. From their discussion it seems that they had been entertained by some of the guests at Noel Coward's luxurious house on the foreshore. The explosive charge was manhandled away from the mine shell and rolled twenty yards toward the sea and away from the cliff. By this time it was 13.20 hours and the sea was ebbing fast.

The covers were removed exposing the honey coloured explosive, a quantity of cotton waste was thoroughly soaked in paraffin at which stage the crew returned to the truck. When I was satisfied that they were not in the danger area I took out my box of matches and ignited the cotton waste. The fire quickly took hold and in minutes the main explosives started to burn giving off a thoroughly obnoxious thick black smoke.

Fortunately the strong wind blowing from the sea fanned the flames and the smoke went up in a straight column twenty yards from the sparkling white cliffs. From 10 yards distance the heat caused my wet clothes to steam so I took them off and placed them nearer the furnace. Within 10 minutes they were almost dry. Removing my watch from its 'protective cover' I replaced it on my wrist and, with thanks to Mr Durex, consigned the 'p c' to the flames.

When I got back to the road and was checking my tool kit a tall young man approached the truck. I could hear his conversation with some of my crew then he came over to me. "Lt Cashford I understand" he said. I agreed that was so. He continued "My name is Lol and I have been asked to see if you and your boys will honour us by joining us for a little drink". He obviously sensed my reluctance for he quickly added that the crew and driver could go to the kitchens with two of his friends who would look after them nicely. He noticed that my trousers had gone white where salt had been left when they got saturated and my jacket was wet at the back which was gently steaming in the warm spring sunshine. I accepted.

The house was superb, exactly as I thought a star of the calibre of Noel Coward would own. Lol left and quickly returned with a lime green silk dressing gown over his arm. He suggested I take off my clothes and put on the dressing gown whilst the housekeeper dried and pressed my suit. He had already put a gin and vermouth in my hand which I was enjoying. Just as I was about to agree to his suggestion, one of the boys came mincing in, dressed in silk shirt and short tennis trousers and accompanied by a police sergeant. "A message for you Sir" he said. "There's an object on the foreshore at Sandgate. The local police have evacuated the immediate area and closed the coastal road." Thanking the police sergeant and the disappointed host and in my wet, salt encrusted clothes, I joined the crew who climbed happily into the back of the truck. I was naive and had no notion of Noel Coward's reputation or partiality for boys, but I must concede that the 'boys' I met on that occasion seemed to me to be very nice chaps.

We hurried to Sandgate where the object turned out to be an anti-boat/tank mine which had been placed on scaffolding along the foreshore. This one had never been armed with a detonator and was therefore quite safe. I removed it and took it with me for disposal later.

After an uneventful rest of the day which I spent writing up my reports, I returned to the Lord Warden, lay on my bed and fell asleep. After I awoke I had a cool bath and then dressed for dinner, another interesting and satisfactory day completed.

What The Papers "Cooked" Up

My embarrassment when pictures and articles appeared in the national press was the most acute I have ever suffered. The whole incident was devised by my immediate boss and his journalist friends. It was the first time I had solid evidence that you cannot believe everything you see and read in the papers! This is what happened.

When the articles appeared the photographs showed officers and ratings eating a so-called belated Christmas dinner. In the first case to have officers and men eating together would have had Admiral Lord H. Nelson spinning in his grave - it was never done. Next, the glasses we were supposedly drinking from were empty, there was never any food on the plates and the ratings were there under sufferance. With the stage set and the make believe feast under way in comes the duty officer, ' "Ten to one its a mine" sighed Lt. Cashford', proclaimed the caption. Rubbish! what I probably said was "What does this s** want". The cameras clicked and recorded the moment the duty officer handed the signal to the Lt. Cdr. "Yes, its a mine at Jury's Gap" says he. What the reader could not know was the mine was one I had rendered safe the day before, an ordinary British Mark XVII which we didn't have time to recover and left high and dry on the foreshore ready for recovery at a later date.

Within minutes of the photographic session in the wardroom we were heading for Jury's Gap, myself leading in one vehicle followed by the Lt. Cdr and the gentlemen of the press. My instructions were to roll the mine back into the sea after putting in dummy detonator and booster container. It was a good dry warm day and I was under orders, so I complied. It took about two hours to get the mine prepared and down into about two feet of water to make it look as though it was coming in with the tide.

Things went well and photographs of the incident were being taken. The Lt. Cdr. was standing in the water demonstrating how not to tether a mine by the mooring rope (a sure way to blow yourself up!) when a wave broke over his back soaking him. I was fortunately on the shore side of him and did not get wet.

After the photo session we had to remove the mine to safety again and clear up everything we had used and were then allowed to go back to Dover to a very belated Sunday lunch. I arrived home mid-afternoon to a very angry wife with a ruined piece of meat, vegetables 'slightly' over cooked (I had said we should be back by at least 1 o'clock). Brenda quickly learned not to get any meal ready until I was actually on the premises!! She was so upset because it was pure fabrication on the part of the journalists and photographers and the following day, there it was blazoned on the front page of one of the tabloids. We both felt there were so many worthwhile things to report without making up stories.

Lost in Norfolk

When my Boss was going on leave I was instructed to take over his area during his absence. I duly travelled to HMS Sparrows Nest at Lowestoft and was billeted in a comfortable hotel.

Three days after arrival there was a call from the coastguard that a large mine had washed ashore under the cliffs at Haisboro and he gave me general road directions to the incident. As usual it was raining cats and dogs and the easterly gale, which had been blowing for two days, was strengthening.

Accompanied by my Petty Officer we collected the car, tools, a map of the Norfolk coast and off we went with the windscreen wipers working overtime. It was soon dark, making driving difficult because still, in those days, headlights were masked although VE day was soon to be declared. After driving through Great Yarmouth and past Caister the weather was even rougher. The rain was so heavy we were obliged to stop frequently. The Petty Officer was navigating and after another hour of driving I became quite concerned for I felt we were on the wrong road for Haisboro.

We turned round and drove back to a cluster of cottages which revealed some light. Putting on my waterproof I ran to the nearest cottage and banged on the door where I could hear a radio playing. When the door was eventually opened by an elderly man I asked where we were (as it was still war-time there were no signposts or place names displayed). His answer "Haisboro" in a strong Norfolk accent.

Doubting him (he was fairly deaf) I pulled out the map and asked him to point out our position. Without hesitation he pointed to a place named Happisburgh, "No," I said, "I want Haisboro." At this he snatched the map out of my hand and pointed, with emphasis, to the name Happisburgh and said forcefully, "This is Haisboro". I think he thought I was daft or something. By this time the rain was running down my neck in rivers so I thanked him and went back to my vehicle.

Crawling along I turned down a road to my right toward the raging sea and picked up in my lights the figure of someone pushing a bicycle which had its lights on. Thankfully I saw it was a policeman. He greeted me with relief. The poor man had been waiting since 4 p.m. it was now almost 9 p.m.

Directing me down a cliff path onto the beach I found a British Mk20 mine lying snugly against the base of a small cliff. Alone with my tools and a powerful lamp I was able to take out the detonator and booster charges. It was one of the fastest rendering safe jobs I had ever done!

During the time it took to make the mine safe the sea kept rushing up the beach and soaking my legs but it didn't matter as the heavy rain had soaked the rest of me anyway. Finishing the job, I collected my gear, recorded the serial number of the mine and made my way up to the friendly police officer who, seeing how wet I was, invited me to his house for a hot drink.

Whilst we dried out a little we drank several cups of 'laced' tea, then I decided it was time to depart. Going out of the door we paused when there was a huge rumbling sound, like thunder, followed by a column of water that rose at least a 100 ft in the air then splashed down.

My policeman friend said, "I knew that was going to happen, its the overhang at the top of the cliff that's finally fallen, we've been expecting it. Lucky you finished when you did because that's just where you were doing the mine". This had to be investigated and sure enough, my mine had disappeared under tons of cliff. This left me feeling a bit shaky at the thought that I might have been under there when it happened!!

It seems that coastal erosion had been going on for years and he told me that in ten years the road would also fall into the sea. He then explained that the local pronunciation for Happisburgh was Haisboro - no wonder we had a job to find the place?!

Unfair Criticism
or One Rocket I Didn't Deserve!

The usual urgent early morning call from the Duty Staff Officer reported two mines along the coast and one had to be given priority. It was at St Leonard's and the area had already been evacuated. Within half an hour my crew was assembled and we departed en route for Hastings and St Leonard's.

The journey (no motorways or dual carriageways then) was uneventful and we arrived at the UXB (unexploded bomb) barrier near the beach. There, with the incoming tide washing around it was a German mine. Working fast it took just half an hour to render it safe. In the meantime my crew had found themselves a friendly cup of tea outside the evacuated zone. They returned just as I was cleaning my hands prior to writing my report.

I instructed the Petty Officer to recover the mine onto the road ready for the truck to load after I returned from further up the coast where I had to deal with the second mine. The truck and I proceeded ten miles along the coast where I rendered safe a French mine. With the aid of the truck and strong wire rope we hauled the safe mine up the beach well above high water mark. We would recover it later in the day to take to the special store in Dover docks.

After reporting by telephone to the Duty Staff Officer in Dover he informed me there was an unidentified object washed ashore at New Romney. I told him I would divert to deal with this on my journey back to Dover. We drove back to St Leonard's where there was no sign of my crew nor was the mine where I had instructed it to be ready for loading.

Crossing the road I got through the concrete anti-tank devices above high water mark and there was the mine, which I had rendered safe over two hours before, floating back out to sea.

Although it was safe it would have been a menace to ships which would be obliged to take avoiding action. To say I was angry with my crew is an understatement. Deciding to wade out through the surf I got a long line from the truck and secured one end to a suitably strong point on shore and then intended to take the other end to a shackle pin on the mine so that when the tide ebbed it would be high and dry and we could recover it.

As I ran with the line towards the mine, which was about 20 feet off the beach, my crew returned. Giving them a quick 'rocket' I then ordered them to shout when they saw a large wave about to break, hoping to avoid a soaking. Sure enough when I had waded into about 3 feet of water and managed to secure the shackle pin and thereby capturing the mine, the crew gave a huge shout that a large wave was rushing towards me. Turning I ran for the beach as fast as I could in my sea boots and thankfully missed a soaking. Two hours later we recovered the mine by lifting it up and over the concrete obstructions.

We then went back along the coast and recovered the French mine. After a long day we returned to Dover, diverting to New Romney to collect a smoke float, which had been dropped from an aircraft. Thus ended, what I considered to be, an almost perfectly accomplished day's work. Before we left Hastings many locals came up to thank us for our labours.

Oh by the way, where were my crew whilst I was elsewhere? They had been invited to breakfast in a nearby hotel, eggs, bacon, sausages, fried bread and home-made marmalade followed by super coffee! Rations?

The sting came early next morning. At 8.30 as I was having breakfast there was a telephone call for me from the Admiralty. Needless to say I was quaking in my shoes when I picked up the telephone. I was greeted by an extremely angry voice "Who the hell do you think you are, putting your crew at risk whilst rendering safe a mine. You are", he said "a disgrace to the Royal Navy, appearing in public with a cigarette stuck in your mouth." I was speechless, not having the foggiest notion of what he was talking about. When I tried to ask he said, "Don't argue with me - you have not heard the last of this." With that he slammed the phone down.

Still steaming I returned to my breakfast but couldn't eat it. Shortly after a Wren steward came in with the daily papers and there on the front page was a large photograph (with lurid caption such as 'Naval Officer Runs from Tons of Death') showing me at the time I was running up the beach to avoid the huge wave which was threatening to soak me, after I had secured the quite safe mine. At no time did I see the photographer who took this picture - he must have been hiding somewhere. Nor did anybody ask what we had been doing, they just made up a flamboyant story to go with the picture. This same picture was later made into six foot posters and displayed in Wales under the heading 'Man of the Month'!

Incidentally the white object in my mouth was not a cigarette but a spare shackle pin in case I dropped the other when fitting it to the small eye on the mine.

Although I had to write a report to the Senior Officer at Commander in Chiefs the Nore, Chatham with my explanation I did not receive an apology. Another cause for annoyance was the fact that at the time of this incident I was a non-smoker!

I didn't, as far as I know, ever meet the photographer but his picture was frequently used and featured in Vol. 9 The War Illustrated No. 220 23rd November 1945. No doubt he was paid well for his tenacity - perhaps he owes me, after all he and his reporter chum landed me in a load of trouble.

Destiny?

It was the third job on this particular day. By 09.00 a bomb had been dealt with at Dymchurch, by 11.00 a mine rendered safe at Sandgate and we were on our way to Camber Sand where another device had washed ashore nearer Dungeness.

We arrived at the Coastguard station and he pointed along the beach to where a dark shape rested at the high water mark. Off I went, equipped with tools and an Aldis signalling lamp. It turned out to be a non explosive conical float which the Germans placed around their minefields to deter our minesweepers clearing the mines. Signalling to my crew with the lamp, the float was carried back and stowed in the truck.

As it was past lunchtime I decided we should go to Rye to get some food. Being well known to the pub landlord we were supplied with adequate food in next to no time, plus a plentiful supply from local fishermen and local residents living near the sea. We were about to leave when a tall fellow came directly up to me to enquire what the device was that had been washed ashore at Jury's Gap. It seems he had spotted it a mile a so off shore from his ex-Naval boat which he used for fishing and he had followed it in, reporting it to the Coastguard by radio, so I told him. I declined his offer of a drink but he invited me to a fish meal with him when next in the area. Since we were frequently in or passing through Rye en route to Hastings or Eastbourne we didn't expect it would be too long before we met again. This chap's nickname was 'Shippy', why I have no idea, he was ex RAF aircrew.

Three days later I had to deal with a mine under the cliffs at Fairlight Glen and on returning went into our favourite pub at Rye for a meal and Shippy was there. He bought beer for the crew and a pink gin for me. Whilst the crew ate, Shippy and I went into a small bar to chat. He revealed that he and a partner bought and shared the boat.

They hoped to carry fast parcels across the Channel and to Holland as it appeared there was a market for such. He had been demobilised from the RAF a few months earlier. Pre-war he had worked for his uncle who owned a speed boat yard on the Essex coast. He was very interested in my work and asked lots of questions. After a while I had to return to Dover so bade him farewell.

Two days later I sent the truck and crew to recover the mine at Fairlight Glen. Later that morning I received a call from the Coastguard at Dungeness to say a fisherman had picked up something in his nets which he brought into shallow water off the harbour at Rye. The net and object should be dry when the tide turned in approximately 2 hours.

Ordering the car I immediately drove to Dungeness but the object was nearer Rye harbour so I proceeded there where the object was still under water. The houses nearby had windows open and occupants were evacuated. Shippy was the first person to meet me. He knew all about the object as he had been listening on his ship to shore radio. He offered a drink which I declined but accepted a cup of coffee. It required a dinghy ride out to his boat moored alongside some piles. The boat had been partly painted and had fast looking bows and hull.

In what was a dining saloon I noticed an Admiralty chart showing the coast from Brighton to the Thames which had markers at various places on the coast. Hanging on a peg was a German holster containing a Luger Automatic pistol, and on a shelf the photograph of a pretty red-head which was signed Virginia. After several mugs of fresh coffee I was rowed ashore.

By then the object was visible two or three hundred yards to seaward lying with the net on firm but wet sand. Donning my wellington boots I walked out to investigate. It was part of a British torpedo firing pistol and fragments of its war head. It had either found a target or blown up on rocks near to where the fisherman had dropped his net. The net was eventually returned to the fisherman and the torpedo metal went to the local scrap merchant.

Going to my favourite pub I phoned Dover - all was clear. Just as I was about to have a gin and tonic, Shippy turned up. I learned quite a lot in the two hours I stayed. His partner was still a serving junior WAAF Officer based at Manston, North Kent. She, it seems, was quite wealthy and was to be demobilised in a few months. Shippy then wanted to know what I was going to do when demob time came. I couldn't answer as I hoped to stay in the Royal Navy specialising in explosives. At the time there was a rumour that the Government of the day were to axe dramatically all forces with mass demobilisation of even time serving officers.

He asked me to consider becoming a third partner in his enterprise - no capital needed only my expertise. I had to leave at this point to return to Dover and he asked me to give his offer consideration and he would give me more information when we next met. I certainly pondered on Shippy's partial offer.

Gales had sprung up in the Channel and I was kept busy between Dover and Margate for several days then a call came, via my good friend the Duty Staff Officer, from Dungeness to say a mine was coming ashore between Jury's Gap and Rye. Calling up my crew and vehicle with driver I gave them instructions where to go and followed in a car.

Arriving at the Coastguard station in Dungeness I was directed to where they had last viewed the mine which they said had several horns.

Half an hour later I walked over the foreshore and there was a British Mark 17 mine which took me little time to render safe. When the crew arrived they manhandled the mine up the foreshore and secured it to scaffolding above high water mark. The truck had engine problems so I sent it and the crew back to Dover as we could recover the mine on another occasion.

Just as I was reversing the car Shippy turned up riding a rusty old cycle. He asked me to show him the mine and explain how it was taken apart to burn out the explosive when it couldn't be recovered. He seemed most interested. On the next day with the truck repaired the crew and I went to Jury's Gap to recover the mine. I was surprised that the 36 nuts on the top plate appeared loose and assumed souvenir hunters had been looking for items. I thoroughly examined the mine but could find nothing amiss. We loaded the mine and returned to Dover where it joined 23 others in the Dockyard awaiting despatch to the Essex mine graveyard.

A week passed and we were once again at Fairlight Glen to deal with a German mine. It was difficult but finally made safe. This mine was not recoverable, therefore it was dismantled and with the crew at a safe distance I ignited the Hexanite explosive charge which burned fiercely. I meanwhile trotted under the cliff to a safe distance from the inferno, returning after an hour to inspect a heap of melted metal. We uplifted tools and made our way toward Rye for a very late lunch. Shippy came and insisted on drinks for the crew and invited me along to his boat.

We went aboard and that was the moment he revealed his 'ace card'. He wanted me to work with him on a smuggling enterprise. They had been doing some smuggling for the past few months. Shippy had a French contact who was a commercial fisherman who met Shippy halfway across the Channel, passed small quantities of gold jewellery, watches, brandy and wine for Shippy to sell to the 'goodies starved' rich populace in London and elsewhere at huge profits.

He then showed me a piece of gold in the shape of a mine complete with horns, about the size of a walnut. It was obviously a necklace for the gold chain with it was about 20 inches long. It had been made by a goldsmith acquaintance of Shippy's for his girl friend Virginia. I had not met her but had been aware of an old but clean open topped Bentley several times, either parked near the harbour or driving to and from Dover. I had also noticed perfume aboard Shippy's boat swamping the usual fish and diesel smell.

Seemingly they had trouble as they had enormous firm orders but they were unable to carry much contraband as it had to be concealed. The Customs Officers were becoming more active. His idea was to carry an empty mine shell in a covered area on the after deck near a small powerful crane, fill the mine with watches, jewellery and small expensive items, run back to Rye harbour at night on the flood tide and drop the sealed mine over the side so that it floated in a normal way, wait until it was sure to wash ashore near Jury's Gap and then report it to the coastguards and me at Dover.

I would go through the motions of rendering safe; I was the only person allowed to be there whilst rendering safe, Shippy would empty the mine case as soon as possible after I and my crew had departed. I would ensure that the mine was not uplifted as Shippy would later, with his powerful dinghy, tow the empty mine case out to his boat, hoist it aboard and conceal it until the next trip. He estimated that four trips only would be needed, each 'partner' would be £250,000 better off and need not risk smuggling ever again.

He gave me two weeks to make up my mind. What would you have done??? My answer was 'No thank you'. Shippy made it quite clear what would happen if I revealed his plans. Needless to say I did not breathe a word of this to anyone and this is the first mention of that 'incident' since 1945/46. I wonder, did I make the right decision?

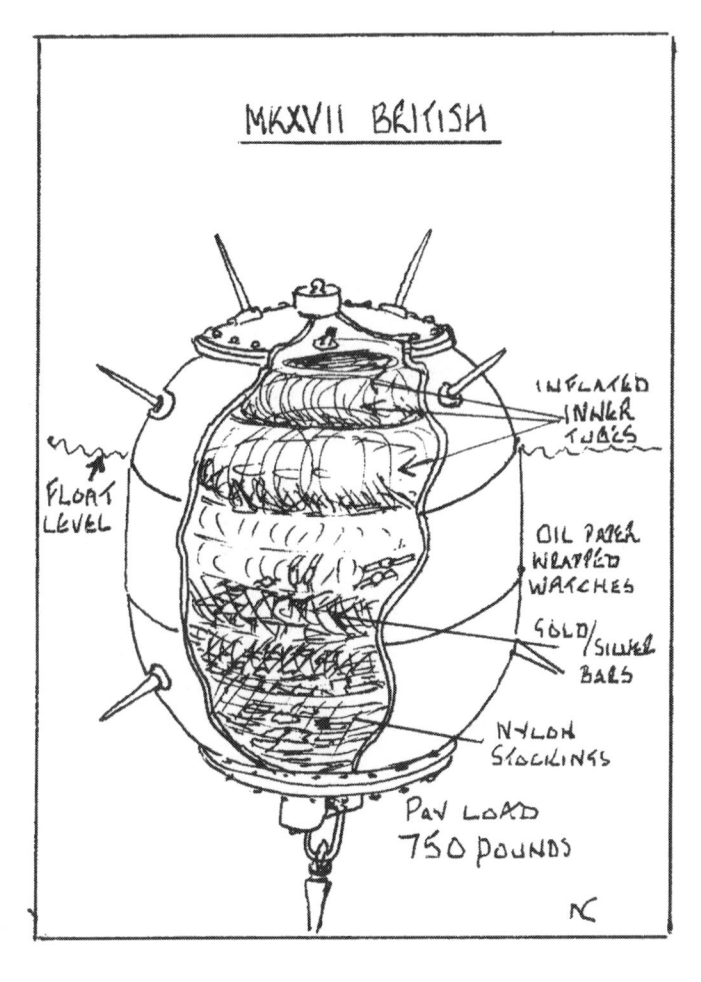

Gales in the Channel - Autumn 1945

In 1945 the autumn equinox brought severe storms with hurricane force winds. One such gale arose during a mine sweeping operation in the Channel causing the minesweepers to run for harbour before they could destroy the swept mines. The tides were much higher than normal and although many mines exploded at sea, many more reached the beaches of the South Coast from Land's End to the Thames Estuary. These mines included German, French, Dutch, acoustic, magnetic, in fact all types of mines.

I dealt with the first mine of a large batch on a very wet, dark early morning (01.30) at Dungeness. I had two seamen with me and we trudged along the beach for over a mile before we came across our mine. Walking with heavy tools against blinding rain in gale force winds on loose shingle takes the stuffing out of anybody and we were no exception. As I remember it, my mine was rendered safe by 02.30 and man-handled up the beach well above high water mark where it would be safe until it could be recovered. I telephoned the Duty Staff Officer at Dover to report mission accomplished. He told me the bad news, dozens of mines were reported coming ashore along the coast previously mentioned.

As he was speaking reports came in that two mines were ashore at Hastings. These had priority as they were ashore on the popular hotel and promenade area and the town was struggling to get re-started with the holiday trade. Any explosions would do untold damage to already battered premises and delay the recovery of the town. We left for Hastings immediately.

Throughout the day we rushed from one place to another, I rendering safe and my crew recovering or moving mines to a higher place where there was no danger of them returning to sea. For days this gale blew and by the third day we had worked continuously without sleep and snatching food where we could. One favourite place was an excellent fish restaurant near the fish market at Old Hastings. Often the owner refused to take money for our meals. They certainly looked after us and we really appreciated it. If you have never been three days without sleep it will be difficult to understand the situation. Anyhow, try. By this time I had seen and dealt with mines of which I had no previous knowledge. I had several near misses and some really lucky breaks.

By the end of the third day I had rendered safe 57 mines, handled countless other explosive devices that had been washed ashore, had six mines blow up within hearing distance and ten which blew up before I got to them. By this time I was travelling on auto-pilot and as the gale had abated somewhat with no more mines being reported coming ashore on my stretch of coast, I returned to quarters in the Lord Warden at Dover. The hotel was taken over by the Navy for the duration. After a tepid (not my choice) bath and three days growth of beard removed, I put on a clean uniform ready for anymore calls that might come in, afraid to go to sleep, in case once asleep, that would be it for several hours. That morning I was the first one in for breakfast and by 8 a.m. was in the office cleaning my tools and checking the security of the explosives store situated in the cliff. The phone rang and it was the secretary to N.O.I.C. Dover (Naval Officer in Command) who said the Captain wished to see me immediately.

Presenting myself at his office he congratulated me and my crew for the work we had done in the past three days. After making me sit and have a cup of coffee he asked what my next move was. Explaining about all the mines rendered safe that had to be left on the beaches due to lack of time and the urgency to get to the next incident and how these would have to be recovered, the Captain asked how long this would take.

On being told about three days he asked another question, "When did you last go to bed?" I replied "Three days ago, Sir," to which he replied, "Well Cashford, as from now you are to take 24 hours leave". Although I insisted it was important to recover the mines to prevent their returning to sea causing havoc for shipping, (for although they are tagged to show they are safe, it is not possible for the yellow tags to be seen from ships, thereby creating difficulties), he was adamant and said it was an order so I had to obey. He told me to pack my bag, take his car, go to Tunbridge Wells where my wife was staying and be back by noon the following day.

There was no way I could let Brenda know about my unexpected 24 hour leave, so doing as the Captain instructed, collected his car (which had a full tank of petrol) and set off with a very light heart. The weather improved and the sun had broken through the storm clouds making the car very warm. I became drowsy and had to work very hard to keep myself alert. I opened the window (even the air was warm), talked to myself, sang and succeeded in making the journey without mishap.

Arriving at my mother's house in Rusthall, Tunbridge Wells I went quietly in the back door. Opening the inner door my mother and brother-in-law were there, he being home on leave from Germany. Both looked so shocked and disbelieving I wondered what could be wrong. "Where's Brenda?" I asked and this seemed to break a spell. Bert called Brenda and she came downstairs. Then it transpired that on the radio during the morning news it had been announced that a naval officer and his assistant had been killed when the mine they were working on had blown up. Brenda had not heard this news item so my family were keeping it from her whilst awaiting the inevitable visit from the police.

My mother and brother-in-law had spent a dreadful morning, trying to appear relaxed so as not to arouse Brenda's suspicions. She told me later she knew something was wrong as the family were so strained and thought she had upset my mother in some way! The sad thing was, if they had told her she would have been able to put their minds at rest immediately as she knew my area did not extend to Bognor Regis where the tragedy happened. After greeting everybody I went to the local police house to telephone HMS Vernon to get the details, the officer who was killed was the one who told me at the end of our course two years earlier that he did not want to be a mine disposal officer. How tragic he did not do as I advised, see the Commander and tell him how he felt - it may have saved his life.

The investigation which followed revealed that several rules had been broken.

These rules were laid down by "Their Lordships" to protect us and one of paramount importance was that a mine should never be approached whilst still afloat. Eye witnesses reported that the officer had waded into the sea and as he reached the mine so it blew up with fatal results for him and one of his crew. I felt very sad that this had happened especially as it could have been prevented. After a relaxing 24 hours with Brenda and the family I returned to Dover and delivered the car to the Captain all in one piece and with grateful thanks.

During the next period of intense activity we were dashing the 80 miles of our area to the west, to the east then back again, often covering the same ground several times a day. The mines and other devices were less than co-operative in where and when they decided to come ashore. A lot of reported items were not of an explosive nature but all had to be investigated, adding to the burden.

It always seemed that the call from the duty officer came just as I was starting a meal and this particular incident was no exception. My crew were alerted and we set off for Hastings as a mine had come ashore at St. Leonards opposite the hotels which were frantically preparing for the first holiday season since 1939. The weather was, as usual, foul with exceedingly high on-shore winds accompanied by drenching rain. When we arrived at the scene the police had already evacuated the buildings and what traffic there was had been diverted. With the help of the Aldis beam light I could see the mine just above the waters edge. It was a British Mk 17, an easy nut to crack - or so I thought.

The on-shore winds were causing the waves to surge up the beach making it very, very dangerous to tackle the mine but I had to work on it. After getting my tools from the lorry I returned to the beach, checked there was no mooring rope attached and also noticed that, on its journey ashore it had become badly dented.

The night sky was unexpectedly rent with forked lightning but no thunder followed and, for a split second, I thought another mine had come ashore and detonated, then came another flash of lightning and at the same time a terrific wave rushed up the beach taking the mine and myself some twelve yards or so up the beach. Another flash of lightning and the sea retreated leaving both myself and the mine high but not so dry. It was at this point that I heard a distinct yet muffled explosion.

Fortunately the mine landed with the top uppermost making it easy for me to place the special spanner onto the bung screw. Within minutes the full threads had been unscrewed and the nut and bung came loose. This was the moment when I turned very, very cold yet was bathed in perspiration, for in truth I should have been very dead, vaporised without trace! The normal rendering safe drill revealed what had happened. The dents I had noticed in the casing were obviously made by a very rough passage ashore. This had resulted, unknown to me, in the main explosive charge of 600 lbs of TNT breaking loose and the detonator had become dislodged and was some six inches away from the booster charges instead of fitting snugly in them. At the same time the battery had been dislodged and its terminals were exposed. The muffled explosion had been caused when the battery terminals contacted the detonator.

My "guardian angel" was surely with me that night. The occasion was celebrated at a very friendly pub on the sea front at White Rock, Hastings and on the return journey to Dover I slept, happy in the knowledge that my adversary was in the back of the truck - harmless.

The Lost Weekend

The night of VE day is but a blur in my memory. Although I have wracked my brain to remember, the memory eludes me, but what I recall quite clearly is VJ night. The night Victory in Japan was announced, I had been collecting mines which had previously been rendered safe and required bringing back to Dover for transit by rail to the East Coast Mine Investigation & Storage Unit.

That evening, after dinner in the mess, many of us celebrated long and hard. There was a south-westerly gale forecast and that meant that a few mines would be swept up the Channel maybe to menace shipping in the narrows between Dover and the French coast or to wash ashore on my coastline. For this reason I drank in moderation, that is to say less than I was capable of, for over the years I had acquired a reputation of being incapable after a mere three pink gins. Even so, if the telephone rang to inform me that a mine or some other object needed my attention, I was immediately sober, which always astounded the onlookers. In the same manner I could be woken from a deep sleep by a messenger to tell me my service was needed and instantly I would be fully in command of my faculties.

During VJ day several of the more boisterous officers had been celebrating in Dover town. One in particular, a young lieutenant, had more than his share of alcohol and was brought back to the Officers wardroom by taxi. He was completely 'under the influence', very quiet but very drunk. His colleagues put him into his cabin, removed his jacket, tie and shoes, covered him with a blanket and left him to sleep it off - the time was 13.30 hours (1.30 pm).

After lunch a message was received that all blackout screens could be removed from windows which still had glass in them. Most of the windows in the building had been replaced several times after shelling from the German Big Guns on the occupied French Coast.

The screens were wooden frames covered by several layers of roofing felt - no daylight penetrated them. Soon a working party was assembled and removal of the hated screens commenced. They did a quick job and by nightfall most of the screens were down.

In Dover town many VJ celebrations, street parties and other events were in full swing by early evening. At 8.00 p.m. a message came through that the whole town of Dover was to celebrate and permission had been granted to floodlight the main civic buildings.

Our 'lost weekend' candidate slept through it all, removal of window screens included. It was about eleven o'clock and most off duty officers were celebrating in the wardroom when one of them decided to check on the health of our colleague. When he went into the darkened cabin the 'patient' raised himself, opened his eyes and looked towards the now unscreened window and promptly collapsed. After a while he recovered and when he could speak he croaked "My God, I thought I had arrived at the pearly gates". What he had seen was the ghostly sight of Dover Castle, apparently floating in mid air, floodlit for the first time in years which gave it the strange appearance of being unattached to the land. He of course had no idea the screens had been removed, hence the shock of what he saw! He didn't touch another drink for a least a week.

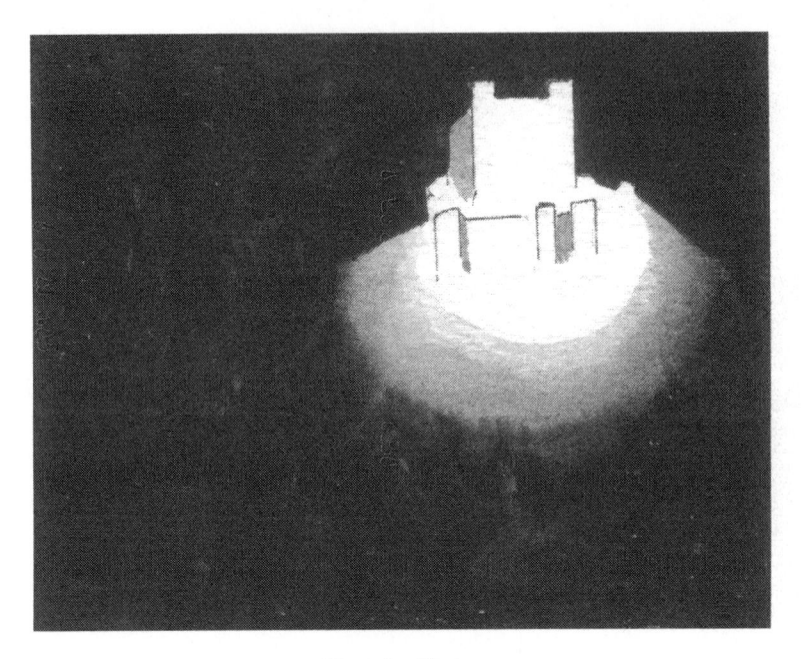

Pearly Gates

Buckingham Palace

I had great admiration for King George VI and always hoped that I should one day meet him. When I received notification that I had been awarded the MBE I thought that day had come, but it was not to be. Some days after receiving the warrant I had a letter from Buckingham Palace regretting that His Majesty would be unable to personally present this award.

My father-in-law was a Police Sergeant at Sandringham during the war and often spoke to the Royals. Later he was stationed at Blofield, near Norwich. It transpired his Majesty was at Woodbastwick Hall, not far from Blofield, and I was offered a private investiture. Unfortunately at the time there were south westerly gales in the Channel which brought many mines ashore and kept me so busy it was impossible for me to attend.

Nobody knew at the time that King George was ill with lung cancer and was convalescing at Woodbastwick Hall from an operation. It seems that later he was not so well and there was no chance of the investiture taking place. They did not want anybody else to do the investiture as it would have aroused speculation as to the state of the King's health, so I had to be content with my award by registered post.

> BUCKINGHAM PALACE.
>
> I greatly regret that I am unable to give you personally the award which you have so well earned.
>
> I now send it to you with my congratulations and my best wishes for your future happiness.
>
> *George R.I.*

22 May 1946.

Sir,

    I am commanded by My Lords Commissioners of the Admiralty to inform you that they have learned with great pleasure that, on the advice of the First Lord, the King has been graciously pleased to give orders for your appointment as a Member of the Military Division of the Order of the British Empire for courage and zeal in bomb and mine disposal operations in the Dover Sub-Command in December 1945.

    This Appointment was published in the London Gazette Supplement of 14th May 1946.

                  I am, Sir,
                      Your obedient Servant,

Temporary Acting Lieutenant (S.P.) Noel Cashford,
                        M.B.E., R.N.V.R.

Dark Clouds Ahead

Towards the end of 1946 my boss recommended that I transfer to the regular Royal Navy as a specialist Explosives Officer. I jumped at the idea, completed umpteen forms and sent them off for approval.

At this time Dover had been almost emptied of Naval personnel, just my Bomb & Mine Disposal Unit remained. One additional duty for me was to collect pay for my crew, which was arranged by Chatham Naval base Paymaster, from the Dover bank. On paydays we were frequently away rendering safe 'nasties' along the coast. This meant that, very often, we were not in Dover until after the bank was closed. If any of the three crew members were entitled to long weekend leave (Friday to Monday) I had to telephone the Paymaster to arrange for a cheque to paid on the Thursday instead of Friday. This arrangement worked well.

Towards the end of March 1947 we were extremely busy recovering mines and attending to other devices along the South coast. One of the crew was due for a long weekend. Telephoning the Paymaster to arrange an early cheque I received an almighty shock. He agreed to send the cheque for that week. The 'bombshell' was dropped. He asked 'what was to be the drill for the next pay cheque'. To which I replied, "We revert to normal". His reply, "Don't you read your Admiralty Fleet Orders? You are being demobilised in three weeks time"!

To say the least I was really shattered. In my lonely 'outpost' I rarely received Fleet Orders. When I telephoned my boss he also was very surprised but told me that the newly elected Labour Government had axed all Navy expenditure and that I had no recourse. One good thing was, although I had been told I could order a new uniform with Royal Navy insignia, pressure of work had prevented me from actually ordering one.

In three weeks I had to report to the demobilisation unit. My civilian suit, food and clothes coupons and a one way train voucher were issued, then a medical. The doctor was a six foot, heavily bearded four ring Captain. I asked if by any chance my application to transfer to the Royal Navy was there. He spluttered and loudly ranted, "We don't want you death and glory bods in our Navy." And that was the end of that!!

I wish I could meet this person once more. I had met other RN types of his ilk before. There was a saying in those days, referring to an officer it was said that those in the Royal Navy were Officers but not Gentlemen, those in the hostilities only Volunteer Reserves were Gentlemen but not Officers.

Anyhow, was I bitter? Yes, I most certainly was!!

Life in Civilian Clothes

Life was hard after demobilisation as a young married couple with a two month old child. I wrote literally dozens of letters applying for work, the number of replies I got was three and these were so unsuitable that I could not even consider them. Apparently the call for explosives experts in the every day work place were few and far between.

Most vacancies had been filled by service personnel who had been demobbed in 1945/1946, so my applications after March 1947 were doomed to failure. It seemed that nobody was prepared to give me a chance to prove I was capable of quickly learning any task.

At last I managed to get a job in Dover. This was through somebody I met during my time there in the Navy, but the company failed due to a crooked MD who took off for South Africa with the assets. Eventually, after much trial and tribulation, I joined in 1956, a National Motor Distributor with whom I stayed for 33 years until I retired in 1988.

In 1959 my work took me to open a new depot in Southampton. Sometime after establishing the business I was encouraged to join the Royal Naval Supplementary Reserve at HMS Wessex. I attended several of the lectures given on board Wessex. Occasionally senior officers from Portsmouth were scheduled to lecture to us. Too frequently for me and some of my colleagues, these visitors arrived late and often it was quite obvious, they had over indulged with the alcohol. They seemed to be totally oblivious to the fact that we had all completed a day's work before we attended these lectures.

On one occasion I raised my objections and received threats from the offending Lt. Cdr. I and some others got to our feet and walked out, never to return. I wrote to the Admiralty to make my and others feelings known, but never did get a reply.

For ten years prior to retirement I had been presenting my 'Memoirs' to customers, associations, Civil Service Motoring Associations, Rotary Clubs, Round Tables, Women's Institutes, Institute of Road Transport Engineers, etc. at evening Public Relations events. I was given a 'Speaker of the Year' award in 1980 at the Royal Society of Arts by the Institute of Road Transport Engineers.

Since retiring I have continued to give these talks, some in the evenings and some during the day. I do not ask for a fee but ask instead for a donation to be sent to Sheffield Weston Park Cancer Care, or other worthwhile charities.

I'm also busy with the Rotary Club of Wirksworth's Aquabox Scheme, (portable water purification boxes) which are sent, via Aid Agencies, wherever there is humanitarian or welfare need anywhere in the world.

Memory Jogged

Many years after the war something occurred that jogged my memory of a strange incident during the war. With my boss and two colleagues I had driven to attend the official opening of a new depot. It was a light-hearted affair and entertaining our customers was very pleasant. During a lull in the conversation I noticed on the wall a large new calendar issued by the Firestone Tyre & Rubber Co., and the monthly pictures were reproductions of battle scenes of ships throughout naval history. The August picture was of HMS Rodney firing a broadside and with an inset of the Rodney shown side view also giving her vital statistics. My memory raced me back to 1943.

A signal received by the Greenock Naval base caused near panic in some sections of the base and I was ordered to board a fast motor launch and speed to the mouth of the Clyde to meet no less than HMS Rodney which was steaming toward Greenock. She was homeward bound from Alexandria and as she entered home waters Rodney had signalled the base Stores Officer to ask delivery instructions for the deck cargo. The reply from said Stores Officer was that he had no knowledge of a deck cargo and could he please have details. HMS Rodney's Stores Officer made enquiries and it seemed that no paperwork whatsoever existed so an inspection of the cargo was carried out which is when the panic on Rodney occurred. The Gunnery Officer who made the inspection of this 15ft long x 6ft wide x 3ft deep crate came to the conclusion that the object was a bomb or rocket.

Someone else remembered that the day before they left Alexandria the crate had arrived on a long ex Luftwaffe trailer towed by an RAF truck and a group of German prisoners of war in the charge of an RAF NCO had accompanied it. With these facts before them it was considered that the cargo delivery might have been a daring attempt, by the enemy, to sink one of the Royal Navy's finest ships.

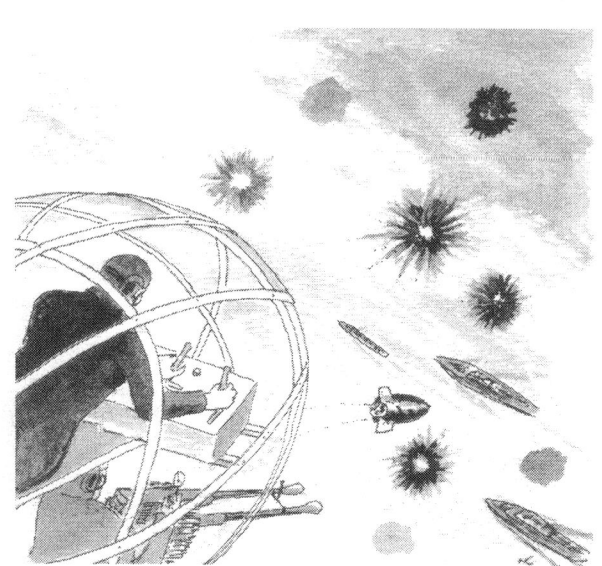

After arriving on board it took me several hours to open the crate and take a good look at the object revealed. Fortunately I had studied every intelligence report received from the Directorate of Unexploded Bomb Disposal and one of these reports suggested that Germany was producing a rocket propelled armour piercing flying bomb which was guided from the bomber carrying it onto its victim battleship or cruiser. The intelligence report indicated that such a bomb would be carried to within sight of the target but outside anti-aircraft gunfire range.

The bomb, which had small wings and a flare which helped the bomb aimer to keep it in view could be guided by radio control and when near to its target a rocket engine, ignited by radio signal would drive the bomb through even the toughest armour plating and then explode in the bowels of the target, creating maximum demolition. Carefully I went through the rendering safe routine, hoping I was making the right moves.

Meanwhile Rodney was at anchorage away from other ships and many of the ship's company were ashore. By the end of the day I was able to give the all clear - NO DETONATORS HAD BEEN FITTED. After this the object was despatched to the "boffins" at Havant so that they could find a possible counter measure.

It was a long while before I heard the rest of this story. An advanced unit of the RAF came across a Luftwaffe stores in the desert. The Germans surrendered without a shot being fired and an RAF Officer discovered a few of the crated objects and was told of their intended use by a very co-operative prisoner of war. The RAF Officer considered that the Royal Navy should know about this new secret weapon, but why it was delivered to HMS Rodney without full information I did not discover. Perhaps someone reading this may know the whole story.

I came across another one of these weapons. It had been dropped near a concrete road in Devonport. As usual a heavy smoke screen had been laid over the dockyard by the time the air raid had developed and a gap in the smoke had exposed the concrete road which, it was thought, looked like an aircraft carrier or large warship to the German bomber overhead. This unexploded bomb was dealt with by a Royal Engineer Bomb Disposal Team. This time I was an observer.

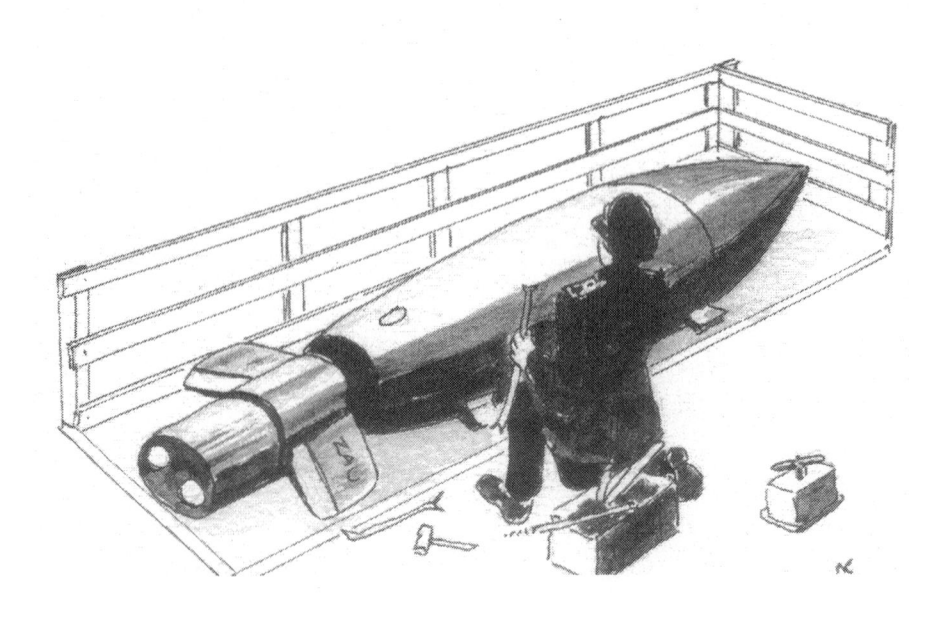

It's All Mine

How did it come about that I give my talks on life as Lieutenant R.N.V.R. Bomb & Mine Disposal Officer? It is one of those "coincidence" stories. An ex-colleague of mine telephoned to ask a favour and I was extremely surprised by his request. He wanted me to talk to his Round Table members about my war-time experiences. It seemed that an old friend of mine who knew some of my adventures had proposed the idea.

This required a lot of thought. Why on earth would anyone want to hear about happenings of years ago? Talking it over with my wife that evening I was not too keen on progressing with the idea as I doubted if I could remember enough to make it interesting. I was smartly reminded that when we lived in St. Ives, Huntingdonshire (as it then was) the purpose built Meals-on-Wheels kitchen she ran was donated by the Round Table, they also supplied equipment such as special cookers and other essentials, therefore it would be an opportunity to do something in return. Deciding I could not really refuse we started to reminisce about those war-time and post war years and the memories came flooding back, incidents which had receded into the distance came back with startling clarity. Fortunately my wife, whom I married whilst still actively engaged in bomb and mine disposal, had hoarded many newspaper cuttings and photographs which helped to jog the memory. Research at the local library also gave me the stimulus to "have a go".

One gift with which I was born is the ability to draw and paint with enough skill to make transparencies (in glorious 'Cashford colour') which are shown on an overhead projector.

The presentation also has sound effects at dramatic moments, this also ensures that nobody sleeps through my talks! Soft martial music puts the audience in the right mood prior to the start. Illustrations in this book will help to give the reader a 'feel' of the subject.

Dates and other boring data have been kept to a minimum, some names I have forgotten and others have been symbolised by initials so that, should any of the relatives read this, old and often sad memories will not be revived.

1987

Motorway traffic was normal for that time of the year and as we approached a junction of the M25, the traffic slowed and came to a halt, slowly moved a few hundred yards then stopped. Cars on the outer lane passed me then I passed them. We had covered barely 10 miles in 20 minutes and the constant stopping and starting was very frustrating. My mind was concentrating on the meeting which was the reason for my travelling to Wembley.

An almost new Rolls had been running level with me and when the next irritating stop occurred I was level with the rear passenger window. A movement from that area caught my eye as the early morning sun rebounded from an object being slowly swung in a small circle. My eyes became adjusted to the swinging object and memory, which had been dormant for many years, came flooding back. The object was a golden ball about the size of a walnut attached to a thick gold chain and evenly around the golden ball were spaced small projections. It was a miniature to scale of a British Mark VII sea mine of the type used in World War II.

A cold sweat of excitement hit me. I looked deep into the rear of the Rolls, the well manicured hand swinging the necklace belonged to an exceptionally well made-up middle aged lady. Her hair was a warm reddish shade and in a flash it dawned on me this must be 'Virginia'. Our eyes met, she smiled and then she too thought of those moments many years ago. She leaned forward and the window started to descend. At this moment all traffic started to move forward and its speed increased on the outside lane faster than I was able to go.

The van in front of me was smoking more than normal and in seconds black smoke poured from the engine and it - and we - came to a rapid halt, blocking both lanes. There was little that I or any other driver could do to help, the van driver was uninjured and after a short time the fire and smoke subsided. With much help we managed with difficulty to push the van across the lanes to the hard shoulder, hurried back to our respective vehicles and drove off.

The whole incident took less than five minutes but I had no further sight of the Rolls. How I wish I had thought to take the registration number! Slowly my mind returned to the present day and as was my custom on trips to London, I stopped at the Scratchwood Service station at the end of the M1 for coffee, half hoping to see the Rolls parked there. To my disappointment it was not.

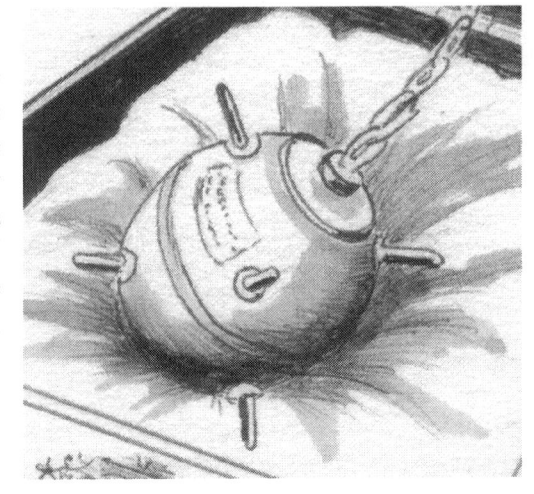

1995 Jersey Force 135

On May 9th 1995 the 50th Anniversary of the Liberation of the Channel Islands took place. All surviving members of Operation Nestegg were invited to attend. The whole event was extremely well organised by the Occupation and Liberation Committee. Also very well covered by the media, television cameras and crew were in abundance. It turned out to be a very emotional time for everybody, veterans and Jersey Islanders. Even the young people were moved to tears by some of the ceremonies.

Many of the German forces of Occupation also visited the Island. I had hoped to meet Lieutenant Heinz Kass who was my adversary when I first landed, who you may remember, did not appear to want to co-operate by revealing what type of mines and where they were laid.

Brenda and I spent a week's holiday in Jersey in 1990 and as a result of meeting a Jerseyman, who had been sent to concentration camps in France and Germany. He was able to introduce me to people who were compelled to work for the German forces. One woman was married to an Italian who was working in a Jersey hotel when war was declared. As a member of the Axis Powers he was therefore a collaborator with his allies, the Germans, after the invasion. His wife got to know members of the German Navy and was a particular friend of Heinz Kass because he used to quietly provide her and her children with extra rations or food left over from the Officer's mess.

My wife and I visited this lady, whose husband had died. She kept up contact with Heinz Kass, telephoning him and accommodating him and his wife on their many visits to Jersey. She very kindly gave me Heinz's address. I do not speak German but wrote a long letter to him in English, hoping he would have somebody able to translate.

For a while Heinz and I exchanged letters. We had a young German friend in Matlock who tried to translate for us. It seemed Heinz used a dialect form of German with which Ziggy was not familiar, so Heinz's letters were very fragmented, but we did gather that his wife was crippled with arthritis and he himself was not in the best of health.

We exchanged Christmas cards, they also sent a little embroidered picture his wife had done. Eventually my letters were not answered. The one I sent asking if he would be in Jersey for the 50th Anniversary also went unanswered. Perhaps his health had totally failed, sadly the association just died. A pity as I would love to have met him again, this time in happier circumstances. I was also unable to contact the lady who had been a friend of Heinz and his wife so even that contact failed.

The anniversary was an ideal opportunity for the 'liberators' to meet acquaintances of 1945. One morning early I decided to go for a bit of walk, leaving the Pomme d'or Hotel I crossed the road to the Liberation Square where the modern sculpture, which had been unveiled by the Prince of Wales, was sited. Deciding to rest

I sat on a seat already occupied by a gentleman who was wearing his Liberation badge in clear view. We started talking.

It was totally amazing, he turned out to be the coxswain of the Assault Landing craft which was the first of the main liberation force to land. I was crouched in the bow of that craft. It was he who had told me, in no uncertain terms, to 'Get your head down' the story which is told in the chapter 'Target - Channel Islands.' The voice beside me on the seat was the very voice that gave the 'head down' command. Of all the people who could have been sitting there, the coincidence of it being the coxswain of the landing craft I was taken ashore in was incredible.

His name is Arthur Willoughby, and after the war, in 1950, he emigrated to New Zealand where he has lived ever since, marrying a New Zealand girl, who was with him in Jersey for the celebrations. I asked him if he remembered the incident - he did. I think it was great that he could order an officer to do something!

Recently I received a telephone call from a member of an audience to which I gave a 'Bombs' talk about three years ago. It seems his father had been in Jersey and when his son mentioned that there had been reference to the Liberation he expressed a wish to meet me. He asked if his father could give my address to an acquaintance in Jersey because they wish to organise a mini anniversary of the Liberation in 2001.

The gallant people of Jersey will never forget those days. To date I have heard nothing more, so whether it is all off remains to be seen.

One day Brenda and I hope to visit Jersey again. Maybe we will.

Lieutenant Heinz Kass

Printed in Great Britain
by Amazon